If you're looking for *THE* book to help you get started with project-based learning, look no further! These concepts and strategies, paired with Lori's passion for the subject, make this a must-read selection for all educators! The knowledge Lori shares in these pages will make your PBL goals seem more attainable than ever before!

**—Adam Peterson, motivational speaker
and author of *Teach, Play, Learn!***

There are many things I love about Dr. Lori Elliott. First and foremost, she is REAL. She is that teaching BFF that you can't wait to collaborate with! Lori has taken what feels like an overwhelming task—implementing project-based learning—and made it feel so doable! Not only does she tell you why PBL is important, but she also tells you HOW to do it! With each project description, I found myself saying, "Oh! Kids would LOVE this! How FUN!" while at the same time thinking how it would really engage students in authentic learning. Win-win!

—Deedee Wills, Mrs. Wills' Kindergarten

Whether you're looking to dive into PBL for the first time or go deeper into your current practice, Lori provides practical steps, strategies, and valuable tips to make it not only doable but fun for both you and your students. Reading this book, you'll feel like Lori is sitting right there with you, cheering you on, helping you implement PBL in your classrooms like a pro.

—Matt Halpern, teacher, blogger, author

If you have ever had the honor to work with Lori, you know that she is funny, creative, and engaging, but more importantly, she focuses on what works best for students (and teachers). Her book takes you step by step through the process of how and why to engage your students in PBL. Lori's ideas and suggestions are easy to successfully implement . . . even in a virtual setting. So go ahead, take the PBL plunge, and watch your students' learning reach new depths of understanding.

**—Melissa Dickson, co-author of *Teaching with the Instructional
Cha-Chas: Four Steps to Make Learning Stick***

This is a book I can put in a teacher's hands and know they will be able to provide their students with an engaging, relevant, and academically challenging learning experience. Dr. Elliott takes what can be an intimidating process and breaks it down into manageable pieces. Dr. Elliott grounds PBL in the curriculum standards and shows the teacher how to take the students to an entirely new level with a protocol that can be embraced and replicated with ease.

—**Susana Lapeyrade-Drummond, associate superintendent of Curriculum and Instruction, Archdiocese of San Francisco, Department of Catholic Schools**

If you are an administrator looking to assist teachers in shifting the focus of their instruction to include PBL opportunities, this book is essential. Lori uses numerous examples differentiated by grade level and content area to get the creative juices flowing. The simplicity of the book provides a framework for teachers to visualize the process of PBL while remaining accountable for content standards, teacher craft, planning, explicit instruction, assessment, and feedback. Any educator who yearns to include collaborative problem-solving in their classroom/school needs to get their hands on this book!

—**Carrie Harvey-Zales, assistant superintendent for Curriculum and Instruction, Plattsburgh City School District**

What type of professional development do educators value most? When they have the opportunity to learn from someone who has genuine classroom experience! Lori Elliott has the experience and true heart of a teacher, which shines through in her book. Educators will value Lori's approach of drawing on her expansive experience implementing PBL across a wide variety of grades to offer readers ideas that they can use in their own classrooms.

—**Shannon Cunningham, national education presenter**

Whether you're wondering where to start with project-based learning or you've been doing PBL for years, this book is written for you. Dr. Lori Elliott delivers a treasure trove of strategies and lessons that will thoroughly motivate your students to reach their highest potential. You will learn how to deliver high-quality project-based lessons while engaging your students in material that will matter to them. Lori's book gives us authentic learning at its best.

—Sam Williams, M.Ed., author and educator

As a classroom teacher, I'm always searching for ways to help a new concept really sink in for students. Project-based learning is the missing ingredient for this! Dr. Lori Elliott's book helped me understand how to deepen understanding, increase engagement, and ensure my students master the standards. She shows you how to do this in a practical way while also including tips for anyone teaching virtually. A must-read for educators of all grade and experience levels!

—Hilary Statum, elementary teacher and author of the *Pencils to Pigtails* blog

She has lived it and learned from it and in her new book, Dr. Lori Elliott shares it! Lori's voice, passion, and practical experience shine through in this guidebook. She provides a step-by-step process that can be immediately implemented and leads to increased teacher efficacy and student agency. Lori helps teachers understand and internalize PBL thinking in a way that impacts their instruction even when not engaged in a PBL unit.

—Macaire McDonough-Davies, principal, Deerwood Elementary School, Kingwood, Texas

This book will help you unleash so much potential in your students. Lori understands the demands placed on educators and walks you through how to successfully implement PBL in your classroom—a classroom where students will LOVE to learn.

—Cheryl Dick, classroom teacher and national education presenter

Project-Based Learning Anywhere

PROJECT-BASED LEARNING

anywhere

LIVE IT,
LEARN IT,
LOVE IT!

DR. LORI ELLIOTT

Project-Based Learning Anywhere: Live It, Learn It, Love It!
© 2020 Lori Elliott

This book is available at special discounts when purchased in quantity for educational purposes or for use as premiums, promotions, or fundraisers. For inquiries and details, contact the publisher at books@daveburgessconsulting.com.

Published by Dave Burgess Consulting, Inc.
San Diego, CA
DaveBurgessConsulting.com

Library of Congress Control Number: 2020948932
Paperback ISBN: 978-1-951600-68-6
Ebook ISBN: 978-1-951600-69-3

Cover and interior design by Liz Schreiter

Editing and production by Reading List Editorial: readinglisteditorial.com

This book is dedicated to all the students and colleagues who have made my PBL journey so joyful and memorable! Living, learning, and loving it with you makes teaching still where I want to be after all these years.

CONTENTS

INTRODUCTION

Have you ever found yourself in a reflective moment and heard yourself say, "Well, live and learn!" I have caught myself countless times whispering this to my wearied self to help ease disappointment and frustration—and to celebrate successes and victories. I've come to embrace this phrase on my journey of almost thirty years as an educator in the context of teaching and learning. I've come to realize that the times I'm most successful have been when I provide experiences for students to "live" the content, which results in "learning." Roadblocks I've encountered can almost always be traced back to not following that mantra. I can sum up much of my teaching philosophy in this statement: "If they LIVE it, they will LEARN it, and they will LOVE it!" This is also why I'm passionate about project-based learning, or PBL for short.

I began my teaching adventure as a preschool teacher to pay my way through college. The lessons I learned in those years would forever shape who I am as an educator. To survive and thrive in that environment, I quickly learned that the students needed to be immersed in content. Every unit we explored included a wide range of experiences, including reading, writing, singing, creating, building, talking, questioning, and sharing. This kept my young learners exploring meaningful tasks, and it was a wonderful way to make key concepts relevant to my wide-eyed little nuggets.

A few years passed and I got my first elementary school teaching job. To it I brought the same belief that the more students lived the ideas, the more they learned, and the more they loved being at school. And was I ever glad I did: within weeks of beginning that first year of teaching, I knew that a project-based approach wasn't just an ideal to aim for, but a necessity to meet the needs of a very diverse group of students. PBL became my way of differentiating instruction and empowering my learners.

I think times are different now, but when I went to college and got my education degree, there were some topics professors just never talked about. They often forgot to describe the realities of the classroom, such as the overwhelming diversity in students' personalities and academic proficiencies. My teachers either underestimated the impact of poverty on attention and learning or simply were unaware. They therefore neglected to mention that because of the impact of trauma on students, oftentimes the traditional strategies and methods don't resonate with students, leaving teachers to sink or swim on their own. I'm always struck by how teachers seem to rise above these types of challenges and succeed at creating truly remarkable learning experiences for students. From that first year teaching fourth grade, I discovered that my life raft was PBL—my go-to method of dealing with these realities.

My PBL journey continued, and a couple of years later I drew what some considered the proverbial short straw and was assigned a particularly challenging group of students who struggled with behavior issues, motivation, and academics. I knew this group was going to be a handful before I even met them because everyone had shared that information with me. They had a "reputation" as resistant learners, more willing to cause havoc than embrace schoolwork. I knew I would have my work cut out for me to reach these students.

One thing I was certain about: worksheets and busywork would never cut it with kiddos like these. I had twenty-eight students with abilities, behaviors, and personalities all over the place. I realized in the first week that I was going to have to pull out all the stops to keep this unique group of students engaged and interested in the mountains of curriculum I needed to share. I looked to my wonderful, seasoned colleagues and recognized that my teaching style and approach was quite different. They were successful with a traditional textbook/worksheet routine, but I knew I would never survive with that type of instruction for this group. I had to make my own way. I had to use what I knew about PBL to guide our learning.

I was sure that the more the students could build, create, and investigate, the better off they would be. The one thing that particularly struck me about this particular group was how limited their experiences were. Most of the children were from socioeconomically disadvantaged homes, and some had dysfunctional family lives. The majority of the students had never been on a vacation, visited a museum, or even had nightly bedtime stories read to them. It was clear to me that I was going to have to teach the curriculum and build background knowledge for everything. The more real-world connections I could make for them, the more they would be able to grasp the lesson being taught—live and learn.

By early spring I had seen considerable growth in my students using the PBL approach, but I knew I was going to send them to the next grade soon and worried about their long-term prospects. I wanted my spunky bunch to succeed in fourth grade and, more importantly, in life. Perhaps many of them would never go to college, but I wanted to instill in them the belief that they were good students as well as achievers! I looked over the curriculum left to teach and started to see connections. I had measurement, geometry, and simple machines left to cover. I decided we would design playhouses to learn the standards. But soon my plan took on a life of its own: because of the students' enthusiasm, we went from designing playhouses to actually constructing one for our school playground.

Let me point out that I knew nothing about architecture, building, or tools. But neither did my students, and they weren't daunted. We joined together to make it happen and reached out for help where we needed it—an important life lesson in and of itself! The students drew up plans, and we voted for our favorite. We wrote letters and visited local businesses to ask for donations and supplies. The students measured, drilled, and nailed the pieces together. Parents and friends even spent their evenings and Saturdays helping us finish the construction. By the end of the school year, the playhouse was completed, painted, and placed in a special spot on the playground.

You have never seen more proud and smiling kids than those fourth graders on the day the playhouse was dedicated! No other fourth-grade students had ever done such a thing, and no other group ever would. (I am pretty sure we broke rules or building codes, but no one seemed to be worried at the time.) It was one of the most authentic project-based learning experiences I've ever organized, and it still makes me smile each time I reminisce.

Years have gone by since that incredible learning experience for all of us, but those students still talk about building the playhouse. They've moved on to adulthood, but the memory and the learning stay with them and me. I had always liked PBL, but after the playhouse I dreamed bigger and could not settle for anything less than real-world learning for my students! My motto continued to impact every aspect of my teaching: "If they LIVE it, they will LEARN it, and they will LOVE it."

NOT JUST ANOTHER PBL BOOK

My gut tells me that you picked up this handy-dandy book about PBL for one or more of the following reasons:

- You are totally new to PBL and are on an investigative mission to figure out what this is really about. You are searching to find out if it is doable with all you have going on.
- Your principal or administrative team has mandated that everyone in your school will do project-based learning, and you have no idea where to start. Perhaps the training you received was an hourlong after-school faculty meeting, or you were sent a website link and a few articles about a PBL school somewhere far away. You are trying not to panic or become bitter, so here you are.
- You have a hunch about PBL and have noticed everyone tweeting about it, but you aren't sure if your vision of project-based learning is correct. You want to clarify what it is and what it is not. You strive to do things well, and you just want to know you are on the right track.
- You have been thrown into the "great unknown" with virtual/distance learning and you are grasping for something to engage your online learners.
- You LOVE project-based learning! You live for this real-world stuff! The more your students design, build, create, share . . . the happier you are in the classroom. You want new ideas and perhaps some strategies to make your units even more amazing!

No matter your reason for being here, you've come to the right place. The purpose of this book is not only to shine a bright light on project-based learning, but more importantly, to equip you with realistic and practical strategies to help you implement this type of instruction. My stories and tips are based on my more than twenty-five years of teaching using a project-based learning approach. Some things just get better with age, and I have found this to be so true of PBL. I want to save you time, effort, and mistakes by sharing my journey with you.

Based on my early educational experiences, I realized that the more students could actually "live" the content or concept, the deeper they would learn the ideas, and in turn, the more they would love learning. This led me to embrace PBL. While this approach goes by various names and definitions, my passion for this type of teaching and learning has been unwavering over my entire career. I recognized what motivated and captivated my students and developed a step-by-step process to implement my PBL approach.

I'm still on that journey. I continue to learn, fail, grow, panic, and laugh each day as I strive to be the best teacher I can be. This amazing adventure has allowed me to teach multiple grade levels over many years and to serve as a technology integration specialist (PreK–12) and literacy coordinator (K–12). I currently spend my days working alongside passionate educators across the country as an educational consultant. I share my expertise through trainings and then work side by side with teachers to plan, implement, and tweak instruction. I spend lots of time in classrooms working with educators and students to figure out this teaching thing. It is truly a blessing to make new friends and collaborate with them as they start their own PBL journeys.

I am also living and learning through this time of pandemic. We, as teachers, are truly experiencing project-based learning ourselves as we search for solutions to educate our students in this new way of doing school. I am excited to share with you what I am discovering about PBL going virtual. Be watching for notes throughout the book and in a special chapter at the end. We are all in this together!

WHAT IS PBL AFTER ALL?

Why is PBL the hot ticket right now? We see PBL all over social media. Everyone is throwing the term around like confetti, and schools are reorganizing to become PBL-focused institutions. Part of the discussion is over the vision of what it looks like, because PBL means different things depending on who you talk to. Now, I'm not interested in getting into a debate over the definition of PBL; I just want to show how it works. Nevertheless, it's perhaps worthwhile to at least agree on what we are talking about. When I discuss PBL, I'm referring to what the world-famous Buck Institute for Education (now called PBLWorks) calls "a teaching method in which students learn by actively engaging in real-world and personally meaningful projects." I think that's a broad enough definition for everyone who is interested in PBL to get behind, so that's what I'll be using for this book,

Given what a hot topic PBL is right now, it might surprise you to learn that the concept is not new. Teachers for decades have understood that hands-on experiences accompanied by critical thinking can lead to greater understanding and academic success. There have been various rounds of popularity of PBL since the early 1900s, when educational reformer John Dewey proposed we "give students something to do instead of something to learn." However, this current round of PBL is more focused and refined. We understand better the importance of standards, assessment, and authenticity than perhaps we did in the early 1990s, when thematic teaching and PBL began resurfacing. After teaching in a stifling era of accountability in the early 2000s, with mandates such as No Child Left Behind and Race to the Top, educators are searching for something more engaging and relevant. PBL seems to be where many are landing.

GET A JOB

Another reason for all the attention PBL is receiving is the world outside the school walls. The skills needed to be successful in today's workplace often appear vastly different from just a few years ago. This is evident in the ways jobs and businesses have evolved because of the pandemic. In a recent article in *Forbes* magazine, author and futurist Bernard Marr discussed the top ten job skills companies would be looking for in 2020:

- Data literacy
- Critical thinking

- Tech savviness
- Adaptability and flexibility
- Creativity
- Emotional intelligence
- Cultural intelligence and diversity
- Leadership skills
- Judgment and complex decision-making
- Collaboration

In his article, Marr noted several other "soft skills" that are necessary in the twenty-first-century workplace:

- Self-motivation
- Prioritization/time management
- Ability to embrace and celebrate change
- Experimenting and learning from mistakes
- Stress management
- Growth mindset
- Sense of curiosity

A big reason why I am so passionate about PBL is the urgency I feel to prepare students for the world outside the classroom. I have no way of knowing what type of job they will pursue, and many innovators point out that the jobs today's students will be doing have yet to be invented. (Who knew even just a decade ago that "social media influencer" and "app developer" would become career paths?) I agree with that notion. I have seen it play out in my own career and the job paths of my adult children. Watching my son, daughter, and daughter-in-law navigate the marketplace is fascinating. So much of their work is connected to technology and digital media. Things change quickly, and their adaptability keeps them ahead of the wave. So how do we prepare students for this type of world? More testing, worksheets, and memorization are certainly not the answer.

> That year doing PBL was the best of my entire scholastic career! I have so many memories that contributed to making me a better teacher.
> —Jamie Warfel Kinkeade

When I look at Marr's list of job and soft skills, I see one overarching theme: these are all skills that can only be learned by experience, not by absorbing facts. There is absolutely a place in education for taking in new information through reading, lectures, and memorization—but then what? To master the skills on this list, students must actually *do* something with that information. "Let's get kids out there *doing* things that matter" is the key for learning in the PBL approach. It's no surprise then to understand the push for initiatives such as project-based learning.

FROM ENGAGEMENT TO EMPOWERMENT

If you want to see what is valued in classrooms right now, go to social media apps like Instagram, Pinterest, Twitter, and maybe even TikTok and search for *teacher, teaching, learning*, etc. I guarantee a million images, ideas, and videos will pop up about "engagement and engaging lessons." If students aren't engaged (the thinking goes), they will not learn, and so PBL often gets translated into "engagement." I myself have transformed my classroom into a rainforest and shown up to school dressed like a pioneer. I have had students recreate Willy Wonka's Chocolate Factory and have made more volcanoes blow up with baking soda and vinegar than I can count. Bring on the fun! Bring on the learning!

The only issue with *focusing* on engagement is that sometimes teachers miss the opportunity for empowerment. It is so tempting when planning these types of engaging learning experiences to hijack the whole thing and just bring the kids along for the ride. They love it, but what do *they* really learn? Recall the definition of PBL: "a teaching method in which students learn by actively engaging in real-world and personally meaningful projects." It's clear that engagement is the *means* of PBL, but learning is the *goal*. So how do we get there?

Something different takes place when we let the students make choices and encourage them to take control and figure out solutions. A beautiful thing happens . . . we move from engagement to empowerment! For instance, consider what happens when I ask a group of students to figure out "How can we improve the water quality in our community?" Students move from simply reading about factors that affect water quality to actually testing water samples, asking experts in the field about the results, and designing solutions for a very real-world problem. The ownership of the learning is taken by the students as they diligently work toward a solution to help their own communities. I see a much higher level of thinking, doing, and learning. Engagement is necessary to hook the students into the learning, but empowerment provides a deepening of understanding and motivation to do something with the information. We want to make learning more than engaging. We want it to be *empowering* for students. That's the essence of what you'll learn in this book—in addition to teaching the content to students, we want to empower students to make the learning their own!

Mandi Dimitriadis is a PBL teacher all the way in Adelaide, Australia. She was a classroom teacher before becoming the director of learning for Makers Empire, a 3D-design software company. When I asked her about student engagement and empowerment, she had this to say:

I think PBL empowers students in several ways:

- It helps students see the real-world applications and relevance of the things they are learning.
- Students are engaged in projects that matter to them, and they can personally connect to what they are learning.
- Students develop skills, concepts, and knowledge as they need them in order to succeed in a project they are working on. This means students can practice and apply new skills in authentic contexts; it also helps students develop self-efficacy as learners.

- PBL offers opportunities for students to engage with their communities, take action, and solve problems. These important projects help students develop as active, responsible citizens who strive to make a difference in their communities.
- PBL helps promote lifelong learning and equips students with skills that will help them thrive in the future. These skills include problem solving, critical and creative thinking, design thinking, collaboration, and communication.
- Through a PBL approach, students can demonstrate their learning in a range of different ways, and teachers are able differentiate learning experiences and assessment processes.

Engagement is certainly necessary, but pushing ourselves to extend the engagement to empowerment as much as possible is the best way to develop critical thinkers and learners! By living what they learn, students truly will love it. PBL provides us the opportunity to take this important step of empowerment.

DESIGN OF THE BOOK

How do we make this kind of real learning possible in our classrooms? PBL can help. I have been on the PBL journey a long time, and the book you hold in your hands shares the highs and lows of that journey as well as my time-tested approach. There are no perfect PBL-ers out there. We are all trying, learning, and growing. This book is for every teacher who works hard to make learning meaningful and rich for their students but doesn't have time to add one more thing to their already overwhelmed schedules. My approach recognizes the need to balance school with having a life outside of the classroom, and I'm here to help you find the joy of teaching without spending money you don't have and devoting more time than you already are to schoolwork.

This PBL guidebook not only outlines the big ideas of what PBL is all about, but more importantly provides practical steps, strategies, and tips for implementing PBL in a doable fashion. Not every teacher will find every suggestion or idea useful to their particular context, but everything in the pages that follow is designed with the intention of making your journey with PBL easier. What you hold in your hands is many years of experience from my classroom and others I partner with, and it reflects literally centuries of experience of like-minded educators who also embraced the PBL philosophy.

In the chapters that follow you see my approach spelled out systematically. We will take a close look at the realities of planning, implementing, and assessing PBL units. You'll see firsthand examples and get practical guidance about how to navigate the realities of project-based learning in your classroom. Chapter 1 (PBL Must-Haves) offers a comprehensive overview of the essential elements of PBL units and differentiates between projects and project-based learning. Chapter 2 offers a top-to-bottom, step-by-step overview of how to implement a PBL unit. Chapter 3 walks you through a simple brainstorming process for planning a PBL unit, and the importance of selecting the right standards for a unit. Chapter 4 talks at length about how to model information transfer in a PBL setting and assist students in researching on their own. The nuts and bolts of conferences between the teacher and student during a PBL unit are covered in chapter 5, while chapter 6 speaks to the importance of authentic audiences and assessment. Chapter 7 is devoted to the habits of mind students need to cultivate for PBL success, and chapter 8 speaks to the questions of when to PBL, and how to fit PBL into already jam-packed school schedules. The book concludes with an epilogue in chapter 9 devoted to PBL in a pandemic and ideas for taking PBL online in virtual instruction.

In short, whether you're looking for how to build your first PBL unit or you're thinking about transforming your unit on the periodic table to be PBL-based, you'll find helpful insights and a useful process in the pages that follow. Along the way you'll also find other PBL educators and former students adding their voices to the conversation as well as snapshots of different PBL units to inspire your thinking and prompt your own insights into PBL.

Let's Do It!

I wish you the very best as you make your way on this PBL journey and hope you emerge by the end of the book feeling well equipped and confident for the road ahead. Thank you for letting me come along and partner with you on this exciting adventure. I would love to connect with you and continue our chat. Visit my website, drlorielliott.com, for additional resources and opportunities to talk more PBL. Use the hashtag #PBLanywhere and share your PBL journey on Twitter! And remember,

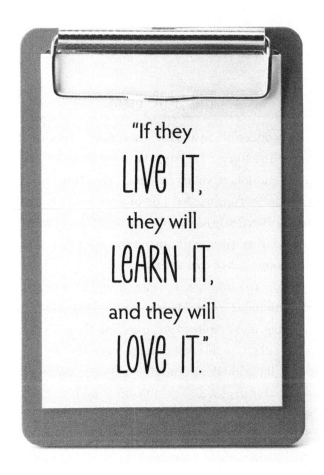

"If they **LIVE IT,** they will **LEARN IT,** and they will **LOVE IT.**"

PBL MUST-HAVES

THE FIXER-UPPER

Recently my wonderful son and his beautiful wife purchased their first home, a mid-century ranch-style home in a lovely neighborhood with big trees and lots of young families. Like many homes first-time buyers purchase, this one needed a bit of work to bring it up to date. It had a distinct 1970s *Brady Bunch* vibe, but with a lot of work they could make it a home. They asked my husband and me if we would help them renovate the home, and of course we said yes.

Now, I have to confess that I am worthless when it comes to these types of things. I mean, I love watching Chip and Joanna do the fixer-upper thing, and I aspire to greatness, but the reality is that I have no particular skill set for this type of work. Knowing that, my son asked if I would contribute by taking down the wallpaper in every room of the house. I didn't have to pick up a paintbrush or build a thing. How hard could a little wallpaper be?

Still, I wanted to be prepared. I watched YouTube videos, gathered the right tools, and thought I was ready to go. But it was clear when I started the process of removing the wallpaper that it wasn't going to be an easy task. Each previous owner of the house had taken a shortcut and simply pasted more wallpaper on top of the existing layer. There were five or six layers of flowers, paisley, and country geese literally cemented together—and to the wall. The stuff wouldn't budge. Undaunted, I did more research, tried different approaches, and finally stripped off all the paper so the walls underneath could get a fresh coat of paint.

It was a lot of work and the result was nothing more than a blank wall, but I felt a deep sense of accomplishment when that exhausting project was finished. My daughter-in-law and I posted the steps in the process to our Instagram stories. I am sure all our followers let out a huge cheer once the final layer was removed. Such a relief for them. (The things we imagine in our head.) But there was no time to rest; we had floors, countertops, and trim needing some love. Another project was just waiting.

PROJECT-BASED LIFE

Life is like that. Once you finish one project, another one pops up right around the corner. We are constantly starting, finishing, or making our way through them. We often juggle lots of projects at once.

As adults we frequently find ourselves needing to accomplish something due to either necessity or want. Once we recognize the challenge, we research and determine solutions. We dig in and work really hard to make things happen. Finally, the project ends, and we can't wait to share our accomplishment with someone else (hello Instagram!).

We live in a project-based world. Our family's latest endeavor of renovating a home is an example of this type of real-life experience. You might find yourself doing something similar or something completely different from our project. But whether you are planning a camping trip, searching for the most cost-effective way to get your graduate degree, or retiling a bathroom (don't get me started!), you are leading a project-based life.

My question is simple: if that's what life is like, are we preparing students to succeed in a project-based world? Are we giving students the opportunity to wrestle with real-world challenges, encounter roadblocks and regroup, and share the results with others? And if we agree that school should prepare you for life, what steps do we need to take in our classrooms to prepare our kids for a project-based life?

WHAT DOES PBL LOOK LIKE?

At this point you may be thinking, "So what is the big deal about PBL? What is PBL? I mean, is it really just doing projects? Or is it more like an integrated curriculum? Or is PBL essentially just a form of thematic teaching?"

I hear you. Educators these days have more jargon and acronyms than we have Sharpies. But honestly, PBL is its own approach. It may have some of the same characteristics as other things we do in our classrooms, but PBL has several distinguishing features that make it both unique and powerful.

Let's walk into K–12 classrooms together to determine the elements of PBL. In other words, what do all true PBL units have in common, no matter the grade level or content area? As I share the following examples drawn from my own classroom and those of colleagues from around the nation, please be thinking about what these scenarios have in common.

Kindergarten

This group of sweet new faces to school were asked to find out "Who are the people who make our school great, and how do they do it?" The teachers took the kindergarten students on a tour of the school, stopping along the way to meet all the important people working to make the school great. They chatted briefly with each member and upon returning to class, they made a chart of all the people they met along the way. Over the next few weeks, students learned about asking questions, being a good listener, and recording answers. Pairs of students interviewed each of the school staff members they visited during the in-school field trip and then created a product such as a video, poster, or booklet to show what they had learned about the staff member and their role in the school. Staff members, students from other classes, and parents were invited to tour the kindergarten exhibit and ask the young interviewers questions about their staff members. The kinders learned about the helpful members of their school community, applied communication arts skills in an authentic way, and educated others.

Fourth Grade

These future entrepreneurs needed to learn a variety of economic, math, health, and communication arts standards. The teacher invited community members who worked in the restaurant business to talk with the students. They were given the challenge of developing a business plan and opening a class business. Students were asked to consider, "How can we open a successful restaurant?" The class decided to open a BBQ pop-up restaurant and worked through each step, from business plan to opening the business for a day. These tasks included deciding the type of restaurant, garnering investors, applying for jobs, creating the menu, advertising their business, determining cost of supplies, taking reservations, ordering supplies, cooking the food, welcoming guests, taking orders, serving the meals, and handling both the order and money transactions. These scrappy business owners served community members, family, and friends, and created a thriving delivery service for school personnel that day during their pop-up restaurant. Students gained an in-depth understanding of economics, mathematical computations, importance of health guidelines, and communicating with others through speaking and writing.

Middle School

A determined science teacher connected with her somewhat reluctant middle school students through the use of PBL. She needed to hook her learners into understanding basic scientific principles about the scientific method and various chemical compounds and mixtures. She began by bringing in everyday hygiene items such as lotions, soaps, hand sanitizers, etc. Then she asked the students to explain how these products were made. When it was evident they had a very limited understanding of how these common products were manufactured, she challenged them to develop their own self-care products to share with the rest of the school. They decided the items must be safe, appealing to their peers, and cost effective. Over several weeks, the students investigated how these items were made and worked in teams to create their own. They produced many prototypes, tested them out, rejected many and started again. Ultimately, the students produced hand sanitizer, body scrub, and bars of soap, demonstrating along the way their understanding of chemical compounds and mixtures. They created packaging, pricing, marketing, and sold the items to students at the school. This project was an authentic way to not just cover the science standards for the course, but empower students to apply the learning in a real-world way.

High School

A nervous social studies teacher preparing students for the state's end-of-course exam for US history and the Constitution struggled with how to implement PBL with the large amount of content needed to be taught for the high-stakes assessment. She decided to have the students interact with real people who worked daily with laws, to help provide a purpose and context for the content she was teaching. Guests she invited to class included lawyers, law makers, community leaders, and police officers, who talked with students about how laws are made, changed, and followed. They discussed local issues that impacted the students and their community. Students then worked in small groups to determine an issue or area that needed legislation or a change in legislation. They researched and created proposals for the new laws or changes to laws. They presented their ideas to a small group of lawyers and law makers for feedback and suggestions. This teacher was able to make the required standards for an end-of-course exam come alive for students by facilitating an experience that allowed choice, passion, and a real audience.

VIRTUAL LEARNERS

Teachers of all different grade levels invited students to choose a topic or interest that they were passionate about and share with others their expertise. Students developed questions and explored resources for answers. They created a product or presentation to share their learning and used technology tools such as Zoom, Google Meets, and Flipgrid to share their passion with other students, parents, and experts in the field.

PBL Key Elements

You undoubtedly noticed several commonalities across the grade levels and content areas in these scenarios: things such as collaboration, real-world problems, community members, research, hands-on learning, and engagement that led to empowerment. All these elements are important components of PBL, and each, properly understood, helps to comprise what makes PBL its own unique teaching approach.

Another PBL teacher I'd like to introduce you to is Tracy Harris, a sixth-grade teacher at John Thomas School of Discovery in Nixa, Missouri. When I asked her what was unique about PBL classrooms, she emphasized how all the different elements of PBL came together when authentically grounded in the lives of her students:

> I find that PBL is really most organic when you can find something around your building that you can make connect with your kids. So, anytime I can pull in a problem that is happening on our campus, something that we can fix, something that we can improve, [it] actually makes them more connected and gives them more ownership in what's going on. I find I can use it a whole lot more within my classroom.

As Tracy and the examples above illustrate, PBL is meaningful when connected to the lives of students, which allows her to use PBL "a whole lot more." Note what she doesn't say—that it's PBL or bust. I want to make clear that I believe our students need all types of teaching and learning strategies. They need projects, icebreakers, room transformations, field trips, experiments, reading, writing, thematic or integrated units, centers or stations, etc. Everything we presently do has its place and purpose, and despite my enthusiasm for PBL, you might be surprised to discover that I don't think all our curriculum should be taught through PBL units. I think we should do lots of PBL, but not solely

PBL. The scenarios I've described above involve some heavy lifting and learning, and we need a balance of great instructional practices to make a school year successful.

That said, I do think we need to choose the teaching strategies that involve higher-order thinking, are empowering, active, hands-on, exploratory, and meaningful even when we aren't doing true-blue PBL. It would be tough for students to live in a worksheet world and do just one or two PBL units a year. Instead, why not immerse them in a learning environment that supports critical thinking, communication, collaboration, and creativity all year round with PBL as a constant focus? That might involve using parts of a PBL approach sometimes while offering a full-fledged PBL unit at other times.

However, doing so requires a familiarity with the elements of PBL learning. What I'd like to do next is offer a systematic look at these elements based on my personal journey with PBL (and thankfully also relying on the work of other educators and research studies). As we discuss each of these elements, please think about how each might be present in other types of learning experiences or structures such as STEM, thematic teaching, etc. It is a good idea to compare what we already do and with things we have done before.

- **Standards and Objectives**: PBL units are (and should be) based on our standards, objectives, and learning targets. We don't add standards to our plans at the end of our planning or try to make them fit inauthentically. We start with the standards! We consider what we already have to teach and what would be the most real-world way to help the students learn the selected set of standards. PBL is not about what would be cute, fun, or cool (although it might very well end up being these things). It is HOW we teach standards and objectives.

- **Challenge**: The challenge provides the real-world authenticity to a project. We think about the best way for students to really learn, understand, and solve a problem or improve a situation related to the standards. For example, the challenge given to the middle school students in the scenario above was to create a safe self-care product other people could use. The teacher recognized the power of having students discover how products were made and creating their own instead of simply reading about chemical compounds and mixtures in a textbook.

- **Essential or Driving Question:** The Essential or Driving Question is written based on the challenge we are presenting to students. This essential question is important for keeping us on the right track with our projects. It is the overarching challenge or problem we are seeking to solve. This question guides our work and helps students understand where they are headed. This question should be student-friendly and easily understood by all. For example, "How can we open a successful business?" is open-ended, but helps students know exactly where they are going.

- **Launch:** We should kick off a PBL unit with gusto, finding ways to hook kids into the challenge and get them excited about the project ahead. Guest speakers, field trips, experiments, video clips, unusual objects, current events, a delightful book are just some examples of effective tools for your launch. The idea of the launch is to both get the unit started and get students excited or invested in the challenge. We want them to feel that this is their project and it is their idea to take it on.

- **Students in Action:** In project-based learning, students DO the questioning, research, creating, and sharing. They provide the voice and have lots of choice in how they go about their work. Although we decide the standards, challenge, essential question, and launch, we must give students ownership of the PBL unit. It is tempting to plan everything out and assign everyone to do the same thing, but we have to fight that urge. Students will be doing the majority of the work, with our guidance. If all the projects look the same, it is not authentic PBL. Keep asking yourself, "Who is doing the most work here?" The answer is the students.

- **Teacher Scaffolding and Conferring**: My absolute favorite thing in the world is to be in constant dialogue with students during a PBL unit. We still teach, but we do so not by lecturing, but rather by guiding, conferring, and questioning students as they work. We can and should do mini-lessons and provide modeling as students need the skills and information. No one is taking a vacation from teaching during PBL, nor are we assigning projects to be done at home. We are facilitating an active teaching and learning experience where we, as the teacher, must be on top of our game to facilitate learning.

- **A Real Public Audience**: Finally, there must be a real audience for the work the students are doing. I always ask myself, "Who really cares about what we are doing and can best provide feedback for this work?" The audience doesn't have to feel like another open house. In fact, I have found that sometimes the best audience may be a panel of experts or a small number of guests who really are invested in the topic and the work the students have been doing. It isn't about just having people in the room; it is about having the right people in the room. Sometimes the audience isn't even physically with us but provides their insights via technology. This has been so helpful as we teach virtually. The ability to Zoom in an expert can make all the difference in providing authenticity to a project. The audience should be able to speak to the work that has been accomplished and provide feedback or suggestions for next steps.

- **Ongoing Assessment:** One valuable lesson I have learned over the years is to assess as we go along when completing a PBL unit. It is not enough to have one grade at the end of a project. To get a true picture of what and how students are doing, we need to use formative and summative assessment tools throughout PBL units. Things such as exit tickets, journals or notebooks, quizzes, reflections, rubrics, and tests provide us with a better understanding of what students know and how they are applying the knowledge. And even though students are working in groups, I stay away from group grades and focus on accountability of individual students.

- **Critique and Reflection**: Truth be told, these are the hardest things to remember to do when you're busy with the unit. We need to build time for students to reflect on their own work, learning, and final products. We must secure feedback and critiques from others in order to improve the products and presentations. Taking time to critique and reflect results in a higher-quality product and deeper level of understanding.

PROJECT-BASED LEARNING, NOT PROJECTS

Well, there you have it: the must-haves, or basic elements, of PBL. Ask yourself what parts resonate with you? What is familiar and which characteristics made you just a little nervous? Still a little foggy as to how this is different from what you may already be doing?

It might be helpful to look at PBL through a different lens to see how PBL is more involved than a traditional project or a STEM activity. I can show you the difference easily by playing a quick game of "Have You Ever?":

- Have you ever taken a shoebox and created a habitat diorama with good old construction paper and Play-Doh?
- Have you ever studied a foreign country and made a travel brochure that showcases your amazing artistic abilities and fun facts?
- Have you ever wandered through the forest to collect various leaves, placed those babies in a scrapbook, and labeled them? (Or if you were like my son, have you ever wandered through a big-box home-improvement store, snagging leaves from the trees in the gardening area, snapping pics of the labels on the trees, and grinning all the way home?)

These are, of course, examples of projects typically assigned in class-rooms each year, and each is wonderful in its own way. As I said before,

I am not suggesting that we stop doing these sorts of projects. I myself have completed them as a student, assigned them as a teacher, and helped my own children with them as a parent (though clearly I could have done better with my son!). I definitely think there is a time and place for well-thought-out projects. My only caveat is that we should not confuse them with authentic project-based learning experiences.

PBL is different from completing projects in many ways. First and foremost, it is through PBL that students learn the very standards we must teach. PBL is not something we stick on at the end of a traditional unit of teaching or add after everything has been taught. It's not the icing on the cake or the reward for having completed the content. Instead, PBL constitutes real learning happening, with students applying the material while they are working toward the challenge presented.

Looking back at our "Have You Ever" examples, one can see that those projects were assigned after all the information was shared and taught by the teacher. The projects would allow the students to show what they learned about the content. These projects were reflections of what students know instead of constituting a process of acquiring knowledge itself.

PBL is different. Let's say you have some science standards about plants you need to teach. You ask your students what can be done with a plot of ground around the school to improve the lives of the students. Through much discussion, they decide they want to grow their own herbs to add some spice to school lunches. The class tackles the task of developing an herb garden. They don't wait until they have read or heard everything about gardening; instead, they research and work toward the goal, learning as they go. This is authentic and developmentally appropriate. A PBL approach cues students to seek information and skills when they are needed while also providing the *why* for learning!

> ## Those hands-on experiences provided relevant and impactful learning opportunities for us as students.
> —Tyler Overstreet

I put together a simple chart to compare the traditional project to the PBL approach. Again, not everything needs to be full-blown project-based learning, but we do need to understand the differences between PBL and projects to help us make more intentional choices in our instruction.

PROJECT	PROJECT-BASED LEARNING
Usually takes place at the end of a unit, after students have mastered the material, based on one content-specific area	Work and learning are done throughout the entire unit and involve more than one content area. Students learn standards/goals/objectives.
Based on understanding and knowledge of topic taught in class; lacks authentic or real-world connection	Based on an authentic and real-world question, problem, challenge, or scenario
Teacher-led and -driven; typically done individually; student works without guidance	Student-led and -driven based on teacher-selected standards and goal; typically is collaborative; teacher facilitates and coaches;
Product focused; often completed at home	Process focused; completed at school
Very little authentic student choice; closed, fixed outcomes with all the projects having essentially the same "look" (e.g. shoebox-sized diorama)	Students make many choices and create their own end products; open-ended results with no two projects looking essentially the same
No real audience for the work	There is an authentic audience for the work that reaches beyond the classroom
Often one grade for the completed product	Ongoing assessment used throughout the unit to check for understanding and provide a larger picture of student learning

The chart clearly reveals the philosophy behind PBL and the difference between this approach and a traditional project or other type of inquiry strategy. Both are important and essential to a well-rounded learning environment, but they are night-and-day different.

What's next? While it might be great to see and hear the results of a PBL unit right now, I have found it is most helpful to walk through a unit in a sequential way to build confidence and understanding. Let's go beyond the theory and move into a practical, step-by-step recipe for PBL success.

LIVE IT! LEARN IT! LOVE IT!

- PBL includes the following key elements: standards-based, essential question, real-world, project launch, students do the work, ongoing assessment, public audience, teacher scaffolding and conferring, and reflection.

- Students learn the project through the PBL unit, unlike projects in which students show their understanding after learning all the content.

- PBL is student-centered with teacher guidance.

- PBL includes mini-lessons, modeling, and intentionality by the teacher.

- PBL Goes Virtual: The same elements are used when doing PBL virtually.

COOKING UP PROJECT-BASED LEARNING

really enjoy cooking. For me, cooking is relaxing and one of the ways I express hospitality and love for others. I may not be a fancy chef, but you won't leave my house hungry! I love making mountains of pasta, dozens of cookies, and vats of gravy for warm biscuits to feed a famished crowd. I can't help but smile these days when my daughter texts me for a favorite recipe. The funny thing is, I have to sit down and figure out the recipe because I usually cook from memory. Things I have prepared a million times are made with a shake of this and a smidge of that. Taking time to really think about the ingredients and the steps to cook a family fave reminds me that when you start something new, you need a recipe. My family and friends love my dishes and want to replicate them, but they need a little guidance.

I have found this to be true with teaching also. We see amazing things happening in classrooms and want to do the same, but we aren't exactly sure how to make them happen. What does PBL really look like from start to finish? We need a little help to get started and then we can do it on our own. Much like how I put recipes aside once I know how to cook a new dish, let me give you my recipe for implementing a PBL unit. I will explain the ingredients you need and examples of PBL units in action to get you started. You can then take my recipe and make it your own. I want you to. Add a little of this spice and a pinch of that, and over time, you will be cooking, or teaching, by memory.

STEP-BY-STEP RECIPE FOR SUCCESS

Ready? Let's get cooking! To keep with our food theme, how about I walk you through the actual PBL unit discussed earlier about opening a restaurant? It is one of my favorites and I think will illustrate the steps of implementation in the classroom well. Even if you care nothing about doing this particular project, take notice of the steps in the process. They will be true for any PBL unit and will help guide you as you develop your own units.

Before we begin rolling this unit out, let's think about some of the key PBL ingredients. First, we must select standards that we want the students to learn. Next, we need to determine the challenge or real-world problem. Finally, we need to write our essential question. These are steps the teacher takes prior to starting the project with students.

- **Teacher Prep #1: Identify the Standards:** PBL units are designed for students to learn the standards as they work through the unit. We are very careful about the standards we select for each project. For this example, we are going to focus on teaching standards in the areas of math, economics/social studies, and writing. The students need to understand how a business works and how a profit is made.
- **Teacher Prep #2: Formulate the Challenge and Write the Essential Question:** Next, we need to determine the challenge or real-world problem and write our essential question. Our challenge for this unit is to have the students understand and actually open a pop-up restaurant.

Our essential question will be "How can we open a successful restaurant?" We aren't sure what this will look like and how the students will complete the task, but we know what standards we want them to learn and we know where we want them to land.

Once we have our standards and essential question settled, we are ready to begin the PBL unit with the students.

When I roll out a PBL unit, I follow a very consistent framework so that everyone understands what we are doing and how we will get to our destination. This example will help you see what a PBL unit looks like within a very conservative time frame of four to five weeks.

STEP ONE: PROJECT LAUNCH

Day 1 (Launch Day)

Once we have determined all the ingredients just discussed, we are ready to launch. This is where your creativity should shine! Your launch will get students excited about the project without any strings attached. When we do a project launch, we want students to enjoy the experience and start asking questions. We know it is a successful launch when students want to know more, solve the problem, or experience it again. I don't tell students during a project launch what we are going to do for the PBL unit. I just introduce the experience and we enjoy it!

For this unit, you could take a field trip to a restaurant. You could have guest speakers from local restaurants come to your class. Why not have a food tasting provided by local restaurants or parent volunteers? Maybe you have a gallery walk with lots of menus that students explore. What will pique the interest of your students? By the end of this launch, you want students pumped about opening a business and curious about what it would be like to work in a restaurant.

After your launch, I say . . . walk away. What in the world . . . ? What I mean is I bite my tongue and don't go into a big spill about how we are going to do a project-based learning unit about opening a business and they are so lucky because they are going to be the owners and operators of a restaurant. Nope. I smile and wave. I agree with them that the guest speaker was fun and yes indeed those samples were yummy. I tell them that I want to know more also, and wouldn't it be great if our guest could come back again. You see, students will start their own conversation and questions while I listen in and enjoy the moment with them.

Most project launches last one day or class period, but for some topics you may want to do several days of mini-launches to get students ready for the unit. If a launch doesn't seem to generate much excitement, try a different launch the next day. We have to get things simmering before jumping into the work.

STEP TWO: CHALLENGE AND ESSENTIAL QUESTION

Day 2

Your project launch was a hit! The students have been chatting about it and you know they are curious. Now, we present the challenge and essential question.

Gather your students together and have an honest discussion about what they experienced the day before. Talk about what they liked and learned. Encourage them to share questions they still have about the topic. Then, share the challenge! I love this part!

Say something like this to your students: *I have been thinking a lot about your comments and questions from yesterday. So many of you talked about wanting to visit or work at a restaurant that I started thinking about the possibility of our class opening our own restaurant. I don't know what it would look like and I don't know how it would work, but I know you can do it. What do you think about opening our own restaurant?*

Hold on to your hat, because usually at this point the ideas will come flying. Before you start brainstorming how to make this happen, ask the students to agree to the essential question. Share with them this guiding question that will frame your work. In this example, our essential question is, "How can we open a successful restaurant?"

Literally post this essential question. Write it on a chart, project it on your Smart Board, post it on your front bulletin board. It doesn't matter where or how, but make sure everyone sees and understands the essential question and challenge.

STEP THREE:
CHART QUESTIONS/NEED-TO-KNOWS/NEED-TO-DOS

Day 2

Because the momentum has started, move on to step three on the same day you introduce the challenge and essential question.

As a class, start brainstorming the questions students have about opening the restaurant. List things they think they will need to research, know, and be able to do in order to open this pop-up business. Have them refer to the launch activity to provide vocabulary and background knowledge. They will not know everything during this step, but the ideas and questions generated will help you know where to start the mini-lessons and project work.

Here are some of the questions and need-to-knows students might mention during this brainstorming session:

- What type of restaurant/food do we want?
- What is the theme?
- What are the jobs in the restaurant?
- Who will be the customers?
- How will we decide who gets what job at the restaurant?
- How much will food/supplies cost?
- What will the menu look like?
- When will this take place?
- Should we think about allergies and health concerns?
- Who do we have to ask for permission to open the business?
- Who will help us pay for supplies?

Can you see how this learning moves from a project to project-based learning with this one step? Because you are asking students what they want to know and do, you are already giving them ownership of the learning. This is awesome!

But what if their ideas seem to be "off the wall," or what if they don't seem to have many ideas at all? Here are a couple of tips for those situations. First, keep referring to the essential question when students seem to be drifting off the purpose of the project. Next, you may want to put parameters or expectations in place prior to brainstorming. This is tricky because you don't want to limit students and have them follow your dream, but some things might need to put up as guard rails to keep everyone focused. For example, if you know your school will only allow prepackaged food items to be served, then you need to share this with students when you begin brainstorming. Finally, please remember that you are the expert in the room! After students have shared their ideas and questions, you may want to also add a few things to the chart because you know they must be addressed in order to meet the standards required in the unit.

STEP FOUR: BEGIN MINI-LESSONS/MODELING/SCAFFOLDING

Days 3–5

Some people hold the misconception that we don't teach during a PBL unit. This is not true. Students need us to present information and skills along the way so they will be equipped to accomplish the challenge. The difference in PBL, is that the lessons are embedded in the unit as students work toward the answer to the essential question. We don't teach all the content and then tack the project at the end of a string of lessons. We scaffold and facilitate as students work.

Before we have students run off into groups or pairs to start work, we need to scaffold the learning. So, what does that mean? Basically, we think about what students will need first, before they start to work. We present that chunk of information, and then they get to work until once again they reach a point where they need some more information, and we provide the next chunk of information or instruction.

Let's consider our restaurant project. Before we can open the doors and invite the guests in, we have lots to do. Here are some things we should probably introduce to students in mini-lessons before they get started:

- Parts of a business plan
- How to get funding for a business
- Job applications and interviews

It will take several days for students to work through these concepts, and along the way they will need to figure out things from their chart about what type of restaurant they want to have and what type of food they will provide. The mini-lessons go hand in hand with the work the students are doing. The mini-lessons continue throughout the unit as students research and need guidance with their work. Remember, the PBL unit is how you are teaching standards. We have to make sure the students have a clear understanding of the standards and can show proficiency in them.

Here are a few more mini-lessons that students would need as they work through this project:

- Calculating cost
- Counting money and making change
- Marketing basics
- Economic principles
- Cooking and food safety
- Measurements for cooking

Essentially, we start with just a few mini-lessons to get students going and then we introduce other concepts when students need them.

STEP FIVE: RESEARCH AND CONFERRING

Days 6–10

By research, I mean gathering information. Once we have laid the foundation for the unit with a few mini-lessons, we have to get students going, and research is the next step. We should not give all the information to the students. They need to dig for it! This may mean reading books, interviewing experts, listening to podcasts, or checking out websites and apps. Whatever it takes, students need to gather information for their projects.

In our restaurant project, students will research menus and restaurants to determine the jobs, marketing, pricing, decorating, types of food, etc. Once jobs in the restaurants are determined, more targeted research can take place for each area of the business. Divide and conquer, if you will. Worried about the research piece? Have no fear, we will chat more in depth about it in a future chapter.

Research is the first step of independent student work. We begin conferring with students during this step—it's the secret sauce to a successful PBL unit, and I am not kidding! Conferring makes all the difference. If I truly know where my students are and what they are doing throughout the entire process, we will have a *Top Chef* experience. If I neglect conferences, we are going to get *Chopped*. I apologize for the abundance of cooking show analogies here, but they seem to work.

Initially, I begin with what I call, "fly-by" conferences. As students are working, I fly by each group, pair, or individual and check in to see how things are going. I will also answer questions and redirect as needed. I don't want to do fly-by conferences for very long because they aren't systematic, and I can easily miss students and overlook content issues. So after a day or two of flying, I begin structured conferences, meeting with each student group during the work time to really zero in on what they are accomplishing and help them as they gather their information.

STEP SIX: WORK DAYS AND CONFERRING

Days 11–15

You may be wondering how this step is different from the research step. I do see them as separate tasks. In research students gather information to accomplish the work. Work days are spent actually creating products, presentations, models, etc.

Students will move through the research and work steps at varying rates. We can't hold them back; they need to go with the flow. However, my rule is *content before creation*! In other words, students must prove their understanding of the content before they begin creating products. I need to know they really have the skills and information needed to accomplish their challenge, so I monitor carefully for understanding of content.

The only way I can keep track of this work flow is to confer daily with the students. I use various formats of conferring to check in with students and see what they are doing and ask questions when they need a little challenge. At this stage in our restaurant project, we would see menus being created, decorations being constructed, marketing materials produced, etc.

WARNING: *Do not hijack the project!* It is really tempting to jump in and fix things or make things your way, but pull back. This is the students' work. It doesn't matter if it is perfect or cute. It matters if it is correct and belongs to them!

STEP SEVEN: PREP AND REHEARSAL

Days 16–18

You can see the light at the end of the tunnel! We are almost there. At this point we have launched the project, presented the challenge and essential question, provided scaffolding through mini-lessons, and put students to work researching and creating products. After multiple weeks, we are in the home stretch. Our guests will arrive in a few days, and we have to make sure we are ready.

Prep and rehearsal will take place a few days before your public-audience day. This gives the students time to make changes to their product or presentation before guests arrive. In our case, we need to prep and rehearse for the restaurant. We need to role-play what each person will and won't do. We need to double-check our recipes and supplies. We need to invite a guest or two to do a soft opening for our business. We want to look like professionals, so this step is vital.

I never want the public audience day to be the first time students share their learning. They practice with each other and a few staff members prior to the culminating event. These rehearsals provide feedback.

This step of critique and tweak allows the students and teacher to fully assess where things are and revise as necessary.

STEP EIGHT: PUBLIC AUDIENCE/SHARING

Day 19

Public audience day is the culminating event for the PBL unit. This is when your authentic audience participates in the learning and provides feedback. Our restaurant guests will be served the finest meal with the best of service. Their comment cards will be used by the students to reflect on their learning. This is one of those special days you are extra-proud to be a teacher!

Put on your apron and grab your menus. It is time to open the restaurant! This is the celebration step! All the hard work has brought your students to this moment. The food is prepped, customers are seated, orders are recorded, and the magic is happening! Enjoy it! Take pictures and videos. Mingle with the customers. Stand back and let your students shine!

STEP NINE: REFLECTION

Day 20

Wasn't yesterday perfect? The students were incredible, and things went so well. Hold on. You aren't finished yet. Take time to have students reflect on their learning. Watch the videos and slide show of pictures you took at the restaurant. Share stories of the fun. Read through the comment cards provided by the restaurant customers. Have students write about what they learned, enjoyed, and want to do next with this learning. Tie a bow on this PBL unit with reflection before moving on to the next great adventure.

Now that you have seen a PBL unit from start to finish in a classroom setting, you may have a better understanding of the process.

Having a step-by-step framework for the actual implementation of a unit will hopefully help you as you design your own units.

- Teacher Prep #1: Identify the Standards
- Teacher Prep #2: Formulate the Challenge and Write the Essential Question
- Step One: Project Launch
- Step Two: Challenge and Essential Question
- Step Three: Chart Questions/Need-to-Knows/Need-to-Dos
- Step Four: Begin Mini-Lessons/Modeling/Scaffolding
- Step Five: Research and Conferring
- Step Six: Work Days and Conferring
- Step Seven: Prep and Rehearsal
- Step Eight: Public Audience and Sharing
- Step Nine: Reflection

How does this compare with what you have done before with projects? I bet lots of the steps are familiar, but maybe there are a few things here that have you pondering what PBL might look like in your own classroom or in your virtual instruction.

Now that you have the recipe, are you ready to get cookin' with PBL? The steps in this process align with the elements we discussed that are must-haves for project-based learning. Essentially, this just puts those elements into action. Perhaps you don't see you or your students opening a pop-up restaurant. I understand. Let's take a look at a few more units in action so that you can become even more comfortable with the ways PBL can be implemented in the classroom or online.

The following virtual PBL unit was mentioned earlier in the book. When the pandemic caused by COVID-19 began, many of the teachers I had been working with panicked because they had PBL units planned for the spring and they were unable to continue those face-to-face experiences. We regrouped and instead had students explore a passion-project PBL unit. This was easily managed virtually and provided the same elements. It was exciting to see this project used across grade levels, from elementary to secondary. Topics ranged from favorite hobbies to social justice causes to solutions for keeping others safe during the pandemic. Some teachers chose to have this PBL unit be done by individual students, and others found creative ways to have students collaborate with partners or in small groups using tech tools such as Flipgrid or Zoom breakout rooms. This example is a general description of the steps used by a variety of teachers taking PBL virtual!

Standards:

- Speaking and Listening
- Writing
- Research
- Content Related Standards (Secondary teachers included subject area standards to align to their content.)

Essential Question:

How can we use our passions to inspire others?

Step One: Project Launch

Teachers showed video examples of students of various age levels pursuing their passions and sharing their expertise with others. They also shared their own personal passions through pictures and videos.

Step Two: Challenge and Essential Question

The teachers and students reflected on the videos and examples viewed the previous day during either videoconferencing (Zoom) or through the use of a discussion board such as Padlet. The teacher presented the challenge and essential question: "How can we use our passions to inspire others?"

Step Three: Questions, Need-to-Knows, Need-to-Dos

The teacher and students discussed their passions and brainstormed questions they had and things they needed to know and do to complete the challenge during this synchronous lesson using Zoom or other videoconferencing tool.

Step Four: Mini-Lessons/Modeling

Video lessons were created by the teachers and posted online for students. These lessons modeled how to choose a topic, write questions, use research tools, and complete the project graphic organizer. The teachers provided students with simple interest inventories to help students determine their passion-project topic.

Step Five: Research/Conferring

The teachers checked in with the students via videoconferencing and/or provided feedback using Seesaw or Google Classroom while students worked on their research. Students shared their graphic organizers, plans, etc., to their student folders in their class accounts for the various learning platforms being used.

Step Six: Work Days and Conferring

Students shared their work with teachers during videoconferencing sessions or using Flipgrid. This provided the teacher with the opportunity to see how things were going and the ability to make suggestions for improvement.

Step Seven: Prep and Rehearsal

Students used Flipgrid or Seesaw videos to practice their passion-project presentations and share with the other students in the class. This gave teachers and students an opportunity to provide feedback to improve the projects and presentations.

Step Eight: Public Audience/Sharing

Some teachers chose to have students share their passion-project presentations through video and others had students share their projects live using Zoom or other videoconferencing tools. The audience included other students, parents, and experts in the various fields being addressed in the projects.

Step Nine: Reflection

Students reflected on their projects through writing and/or video. They shared what they had learned and reflected on the feedback received. They wrote thank you notes to audience members.

The passion-project PBL was for many the first attempt at taking PBL virtual and I am so pleased to say that it worked! Students were able to have choice, explore, create, and share with authentic audiences. This convinced me that PBL can be effective in a virtual environment. We may use different tools, but our purpose and steps remain the same. Is this the most perfect PBL unit? Perhaps not, but there is no perfect PBL unit. We live and learn as we go, and pivot to meet the needs of students.

Let's explore another PBL unit. This one was completed by some high school teachers I worked with recently in South Carolina. This project was designed to meet a set of standards taught by algebra and geometry teachers. Here is a quick snapshot of the project implemented in the classroom, step-by-step:

SCHOOL-IMPROVEMENT PROJECT

Students were challenged to find solutions for the lack of school facilities for additional extracurricular activities. Students researched and designed solutions, working within a budget. They created models, diagrams, reports, and formal presentations for each of the solutions. They presented their findings to the superintendent and school board as possible improvements for the school.

Standards:

- Algebraic formulas
- Budgeting
- Measurement
- Application of geometry

Essential Question:

How can we improve our school facilities to involve more students in extracurricular activities?

Step One: Project Launch

The teachers used the celebration of the basketball team going to state as a launch for the project discussion. They asked students what other sports, activities, or clubs they would like to see succeed at a high level. Then they asked about the obstacles to this success.

Step Two: Challenge and Essential Question

Based on the interest and discussion with students, the teachers challenged students to select a school-improvement project that would benefit the students and allow them to be successful.

"How can we improve our school facilities to involve more students in extracurricular activities?"

Step Three: Chart Questions/Need-to-Knows/ Need-to-Dos

The students brainstormed options for improvement such as adding a pool, track, baseball field, etc. They agreed to survey students and parents to see which one would be most beneficial.

Step Four: Mini-Lessons/Modeling

Teachers shared mini-lessons on creating and analyzing data, on math for determining price of each of the suggested improvements, on measurement, formulas, etc.

Step Five: Research/Conferring

Students worked on collecting data, analyzing data, and selecting a project focus. Then they determined the actual cost of the construction. They interviewed experts, community leaders, school leaders, etc.

Step Six: Work Days and Conferring

Each group of students handled a different part of the project. Models, digital presentations, and face-to-face presentations were created/ produced.

Step Seven: Prep and Rehearsal

Students rehearsed presentations in class and received feedback, stayed after school to set up their displays, then practiced by presenting to school faculty members.

Step Eight: Public Audience/Sharing

The students presented their findings to the superintendent, leadership team, and school board, and parents at a PBL Night.

Step Nine: Reflection

Students completed oral and written reflections on the project.

My guess is you were able to read through this recent example more easily than the first. Not only because of less text, but your understanding of the PBL process is much stronger. You will make this your own, of course, but a step-by-step guide can be very helpful when trying to navigate your own PBL unit. Here are a few more examples just to solidify the steps and share some fun project ideas.

PROJECT PET CARE (ELEMENTARY)

Students in Monett, Missouri, were concerned about the possible closing of an animal shelter in the community. They were challenged to find a way to teach community members and other students about proper pet care. They also decided to collect donations for the animal shelter in jeopardy.

Standards:

- Animals
- How-to writing
- Research

Essential Question:

How can we teach others about pet care?

Step One: Project Launch

Guests who train service animals visited the classroom and shared tips on pet care. A volunteer from the animal shelter spoke about their work and how they cared for animals.

Step Two: Challenge and Essential Question

Students were presented with the challenge and the essential question was discussed and posted: How can we teach others about pet care?

Step Three: Chart Questions/Need-to-Knows/Need-to-Dos

Students brainstormed and discussed questions they had about the topic, things they needed to know, and things they needed to do to meet the challenge. The class created a chart of responses that they would use throughout the unit.

Step Four: Provide Mini-Lessons and Modeling

Initial mini-lessons included vocabulary related to pet care and how to find information from resources and complete the graphic organizer.

Step Five: Research and Conferring

Students began researching pets and pet care. More special guests/experts spoke to students about pet care, and conferences with students began.

Step Six: Work Days and Conferring

Mini-lessons about how-to writing began as research was being completed. Students chose and planned how to teach others about pet care and created some type of how-to writing. They created a product or presentation to teach others about pet care. Conferences continued throughout the selection, planning, and creating phases.

Step Seven: Prep and Rehearsal

Three to four days prior to public audience day students shared with another group and received feedback. Then they presented to the teacher and other faculty members for more feedback. They tweaked products and presentations based upon feedback.

Step Eight: Public Audience and Sharing

Students displayed their pet-care products and shared with students, expert guests, and parents. They collected donations for the animal shelter.

Step Nine: Reflection

Students completed a written reflection including what they had learned and how their work impacted others. The class discussed the experience and learning. Donations were taken to the animal shelter.

CULTURAL COOKBOOK (MIDDLE SCHOOL)

Students in South Carolina were challenged to learn more about cultural diversity within their own community. They were asked to determine a way to celebrate this diversity by creating a written product they could share with an authentic audience. Ultimately, the students decided they would publish a class book of recipes from various cultures to share at their local community festival.

Standards:

- Writing process
- Countries and cultures

Essential Question:

How can we celebrate our cultural diversity through writing?

Step One: Project Launch

The class had a food tasting of dishes prepared by students and their families. Students had discussions about diversity with school staff members from various countries.

Step Two: Challenge and Essential Question

Students decided to focus on the foods of each culture by making a cookbook of recipes to sell or give away at the festival. The essential question, How can we celebrate our cultural diversity through writing? was shared and posted.

Step Three: Chart Questions/Need-to-Knows/Need-to-Dos

Students brainstormed and discussed questions they have about the topic, things they need to know, and things they need to do to meet the challenge. A chart of responses was created to use throughout the unit.

Step Four: Provide Mini-Lessons and Modeling

Initial mini-lessons included "What is cultural diversity?" and "How are cookbooks organized and written?"

Step Five: Research and Conferring

Students researched cultures and countries represented in their community. Special guests/experts were invited to speak with students about their cultures and recipes. Conferences with students about topic selection and research began.

Step Six: Work Days and Conferring

Mini-lessons in the writing process were shared. Students decided on the type of cookbook and designated sections to groups, which gathered and organized recipes. Students wrote descriptions for each recipe and created the cookbook using an online publishing tool. Conferences with students continued throughout the selection, planning, and creating phases. Students also planned and created items for the festival booth.

Step Seven: Prep and Rehearsal

Three to four days prior to the festival, students shared the work with other groups and presented the cookbook draft to the teacher or other faculty members for feedback. Then they tweaked the cookbook based upon feedback received.

Step Eight: Public Audience and Sharing

Students intended to attend the festival and share the cookbook with patrons. (Reality: The students ran into a time crunch completing the cookbook by the time of the festival. They were unable to share at the event but made the cookbooks available to students and staff instead.

Sometimes, even with our best plans, we have to change directions because life happens and that is okay.)

Step Nine: Reflection

Students completed a written reflection including what they learned and how their work might impact others, then discussed as a class the process and the learning.

For years teachers would ask me about my project-based learning units and how my students accomplished so much. I had to really sit down and reflect on my own instruction. What did I do to structure our units so that students did succeed and still have ownership of the learning? What mistakes had I made in the past that caused a less than productive unit or ended with students still unsure of the standards? Once I pondered my own practice, I recognized the nine steps I just shared. I applied these same nine steps in every successful project-based learning unit I have designed.

Just like we adjust and add to recipes once we understand the basics of cooking a dish, we adjust and add to our project-based learning units with each experience. But at this point you are probably thinking, *this is great, but how does it really work*? What about assessment, management, and TIME? Take a deep breath. I have got you covered. I have also struggled with the very things you are worried about, and I am excited to share some ideas that will ease your mind and help you with reality checks each step of the way. Stick with me and let's get real about how to plan and implement PBL.

LIVE IT! LEARN IT! LOVE IT!

Implementing a PBL unit in the classroom typically involves the following step-by-step approach:

- Prior to the PBL Unit
    - Teacher Prep #1: Identify the Standards
    - Teacher Prep #2: Formulate the Challenge and Write the Essential Question

- Rollout in the Classroom
    - Step One: Project Launch
    - Step Two: Challenge and Essential Question
    - Step Three: Chart Questions/Need-to-Knows/ Need-to-Do
    - Step Four: Begin Mini-Lessons/Modeling/Scaffolding
    - Step Five: Research and Conferring
    - Step Six: Workdays and Conferring
    - Step Seven: Prep and Rehearsal
    - Step Eight: Public Audience and Sharing
    - Step Nine: Reflection

- PBL Goes Virtual: We use the same steps for implementing PBL in virtual instruction, but we use student-friendly technology to assist us, such as Seesaw, Google Classroom, Zoom, Flipgrid, etc.

PLANNING FOR PBL

N ow that we have seen PBL in action in classrooms from kindergarten to high school, let's tackle the planning process for PBL units.

Lesson plans. Love them or hate them, they are part of the teaching game. What is your lesson planning style?

   a. Lesson plans? What lesson plans? I just show up and the magic happens.
   b. I am a big-picture person. I know basically where I am headed and fill in the details as we go. I write basic notes to remind myself of what is ahead.
   c. Have you seen my binder? I have every minute of every day mapped out. My plans are aligned to standards, color coded, and tabbed.
   d. I am totally comfortable using the district's online lesson-plan form. The more check boxes, the better.

There is obviously no one way to brainstorm and plan lessons. The same is true with PBL. There isn't a perfect template or system that works for everyone. I won't try to change how you plan and prioritize, but I would like to offer an approach to PBL planning that will guide you from brainstorming to actual daily plans. My reasoning is simple.

Many teachers I work with struggle with the ownership of PBL. They aren't sure how to develop their own units. I know it can seem daunting, so let me share with you how I work through this process. Feel free to adjust steps to work better for you and your planning style.

BRAINSTORMING A NEW UNIT

"Lori, where do you come up with ideas for projects?" I am asked this all the time. I use a four-step process for brainstorming that helps me get the juices going. This graphic organizer helps me arrange my thoughts:

1. Standards I Need to Teach	2. What Does This Look Like in the Real World?
3. "What If?" Project Ideas	4. Resources I Already Have

BRAINSTORMING STEP ONE: STANDARDS I NEED TO TEACH

There was a time when standards and objectives were housed in giant red binders and placed on a shelf to collect dust. These red binders served as just another stack of paperwork to appease the state department of education folks who would drop by occasionally to see if we had all our ducks in a row. Things changed as we moved into the accountability phase of education with No Child Left Behind. The red binders were replaced with shiny new standards and student outcome goals neatly printed on large sheets of blue paper, affectionately called placemats.

New assessments were designed to align with the lofty goals typed on the placemats. The ultimate hope was that students would be able to demonstrate their mastery of the standards on the placemat. As difficult as it was to transition from total freedom to a standards-based focus, I can honestly say that I am a much better teacher because of it. I may not agree with all the standards and where they fall developmentally, but in terms of intentional instruction, they have helped me tremendously. I now understand what I need to teach and how it will be assessed. My PBL units are much more rigorous now because of the focus on standards. I know we are tired of hearing about rigor, but the higher expectations in curricula have raised the bar for thinking and learning in project-based learning classrooms.

STANDARDS, OBJECTIVES, AND CURRICULUM . . . OH MY!

Choosing standards for our units is much more than trying to leave a paper trail. PBL is HOW we learn the standards, not an extra activity. So, we have to be really picky about which curriculum targets/objectives we select. I recently visited with an instructional coach who asked me if I always started with the standards when planning a PBL unit. She expressed that she felt that teachers could start with a project idea and then "make the standards fit." We had a great conversation about how both mindsets play out. I shared with her that I found if I simply start with a fun or engaging idea for a project, I find myself picking random standards that seem to go with my vision, but the focus is less on the standards than the activity. This often leads to what I call PBL fluff-and-stuff. In other words, we spend weeks working on something that is engaging and fun, but at the end we aren't really sure what the students have learned.

I prefer to start with something I have already been handed and am expected to teach and that the students are expected to master before leaving my classroom. When taking a deep dive into my standards/objectives, I select what I call the "big rocks" for my course, grade level, or content area. I really look at which standards are most important for students to master. Which ones are they assessed on, on the state assessment? Which are the nonnegotiables? In other words, which standards are on my shoulders for the students to understand and apply? I discussed with this new friend how selecting standards first keeps me true to my curriculum and focused on the appropriate learning. I do fully recognize that sometimes a creative idea is so powerful we may start with what we want the students to experience and then select standards, but I always want to be mindful of my real curriculum standards when brainstorming a new unit.

My colleague Tracy Harris puts it this way:

> You have to tie in your standards. You have to know what standards you want to address during the project-based activity or project so you have accountability as to what you are trying to accomplish. Again, it has been very easy to find things around our school that go along with what we are teaching. If you can find something that is truly meaningful that's happening for you and your students, you will be able to find standards within your core subject areas to fit into what you are trying to accomplish.

> Look around your campus. Is there anything that you can turn into a problem that could be easily solved? How does that tie into the standards you are teaching? It is more of a backward design. What is your end purpose? What steps will get your kids there? You have to understand what you want from it, and these are the things that have to happen in order for you to be successful.

Let's say I am a middle school science teacher and I love teaching about space. I personally love the stars, planets, simulations of Space Camp, making solar system models, etc. I teach eighth grade and have a few standards in my science curriculum related to space, but it is really taught in depth in sixth grade. I could design a PBL unit related to space that teaches my two tiny standards, and my students will enjoy building the next rocket to Mars, but it will take weeks and

I have clusters of other standards that are more pressing for my grade level, including focusing on matter and how matter interacts. The matter standards are my big rocks. I choose to put my energy into a PBL unit about matter rather than rehash concepts about space that students have already experienced.

Standards are not all created equal. Some are to be introduced, or to be explored, analyzed, and applied. Still others are to be reviewed and built upon. To do quality PBL work, we must take time to examine our standards and curriculum objectives. We must know what we are supposed to teach and to what depth. We want to get the most bang for our buck, so we select strands and clusters of standards that are must-haves for our grade levels or courses. This helps us address assessment needs and justify the amount of time spent on the units.

When I asked Mandi Dimitriadis about standards and the curriculum, she shared this insight:

> I think PBL is a very rewarding way to teach, as teachers can see students achieving real outcomes in projects that matter to them. This approach frees teachers up to design meaningful, relevant, and engaging learning experiences for their students. They can meet curriculum outcomes without being slaves to covering curriculum content step by step. I think of this approach as "uncovering the curriculum" rather than "covering the curriculum." By this I mean that PBL allows teachers to focus on the big conceptual ideas in the curriculum and use rich, engaging projects to help students develop knowledge and skills rather than teaching knowledge and skills in isolation. This also helps teachers navigate their way through a crowded curriculum, as they can address outcomes from different curriculum areas through the one project.

Here are my tips for selecting standards for units:

1. Choose the BIG ROCKS! Choose the standards that you want students to understand and that should be explored, analyzed,

and applied! Take a little time to look at the curriculum in the grades or courses before and after your grade level or course. Are the same standards listed across the levels? Are ideas or skills added each year to the cluster of standards or do they stand alone? Who should be shouldering the weight of the standards?

2. Look for clusters of standards in a subject area that make sense together. We want to build our PBL units on more than one or two standards, so look for a hearty cluster! Some curriculum guides call these threads or strands. We need enough content to keep students thinking and wrestling with ideas, so look for clusters that tie ideas together.

3. Choose standards that authentically connect with other content areas. Consider how the standards look when in motion in the real world. If you want to teach measurement in our math instruction, it might make sense to also learn about the design process in science and presentation skills in communication arts.

4. Be Goldilocks! You know the story . . . too big, too small, just right? Selecting standards can be like a trip to the three bears' house. We pick any standard or content idea that seems to match the project—too big. Or we might get laser focused on just one or two standards and that might not be the best use of time—too small. So be Goldilocks . . . you want the just right number of standards that you can realistically address and assess through the project. There is no magic number of standards or objectives for each unit, but I try to keep myself in the range of three to six per content area being addressed in the unit.

5. Ask yourself the hard question, "Are these standards worthy of the time involved in this project?" If the standards you want to address can easily be taught in one lesson or a few activities, then pass on those standards. Search for the standards that are worthy of the time and effort you and your students will put forth in the unit.

Essential Question: How can we make our new neighbors feel welcome in our city?

Content Areas: Social Studies, Communication Arts

Students were challenged to help new residents to their community feel welcome and informed about the special features of the city. Students researched the history of the city and interviewed community leaders to learn about the services and opportunities available. The students put together marketing and welcome packets to share with potential and new residents. They partnered with the chamber of commerce to disperse the materials.

MIDDLE SCHOOL – PBL UNIT –

As I said, the starting point is the standards kids need to learn. I look through my standards and decide what clusters of standards I want to address in the unit. Remember, selection of standards is vital for a content-rich unit, so I think about what standards I most want students to know, understand, and apply. I am looking for connections across content areas and heavy-hitting objectives that will provide opportunity for deep understanding and authentic learning. The standards/objectives are not optional—I am required to teach them. Why not choose the most interesting ones for my PBL units?

BRAINSTORMING STEP TWO: WHAT DOES THIS LOOK LIKE IN THE REAL WORLD

Once I have standards in mind, I take off my teacher hat and think outside the classroom—like a real person, not a teacher. I know we are also real people, but we do get caught in our own little bubbles and think in terms of research papers, posters, and brochures. I try hard to go outside my comfort zone and dream big. I ask myself, "Who in the world really does this stuff?" and "Who uses these standards in everyday life or where do I see them being exhibited in the real world?" Press pause. Sometimes I don't know how the standards are used outside of education. I must do some quick research, ask a friend, or clarify my own misunderstandings.

Some of my best PBL pals choose to start at step two and move back to step one in brainstorming. They look around their school, community, or nation to find things that need to be changed or improved. I say, "Bravo!" I love the community and world connections. My only hesitation is when we focus solely on the project we want completed and then try to slide in the standards as an afterthought (the PBL fluff-and-stuff concern I mentioned before). This approach makes me, personally, nervous. I am pretty sure this comes from having taught for so many years in a standards-driven, test-scores-matter, district.

There have been times when a current event or community need propelled me into a PBL unit, and I searched for the standards to make it happen. However, over the years I have become more in tune with my curriculum and standards and choose to start with my objectives so I am not trying to make standards fit inauthentically.

BRAINSTORMING STEP THREE: "WHAT IF?" PROJECT IDEAS

Now the fun begins! Based on a real-world scenario I've identified, I start thinking about projects we can do. What if we plant a garden and feed the homeless? What if we design a playground that would help children with special needs? What if we connected with students in another state and learned about the regions and characteristics of our communities? What if we published books to teach younger children about bullying?

I refer to this step of brainstorming as the "dating phase." We are just dating ideas here, and we don't have to put a ring on it yet. The more I think, talk with others, and flesh out my "what if?" ideas, the closer I get to "marrying" one. I narrow my "what if" ideas down to one or two and move to the final brainstorming phase.

BRAINSTORMING STEP FOUR: RESOURCES I ALREADY HAVE

This is the reality-check step. I consider my "what if" project idea and list all the resources I already have or could have to do this PBL unit with my students. Who do I know? What technology is available? How can I make this happen virtually if necessary? What funding is available? How could we get funding and experts to help? I don't have to have everything ready to go, but I think through how we might access the things we need to make the unit happen.

Once I reach this step, I either have a gut feeling that this PBL unit idea will work, or that I need to trash it and try something else. I suggest to teachers that once they work through these steps and feel they have pinned down the direction of the unit, they should put the plan away for a day. Walk away for a little bit. If you still like the idea when you look at it again, then "marry" it. If not, go back to the drawing board and know that a little trial and error is OK.

What might this process look like in action? Here is an idea generator that shows the results from some of my brainstorming for various standards I needed to address over the years. Perhaps one of the ideas will resonate with you as you start thinking about your next PBL unit.

STANDARDS	CHALLENGE/ROLE	PRODUCT/PUBLIC AUDIENCE
Economics Money Life Skills	Open a business: restaurant, store, etc.	Run a business and invite others to be patrons of the business
Measurement Budgets Engineering	Become architects, contractors, or designers	Create/build models or actual size structures, share with actual architects, contractors, etc.
Animals/ Habitats Landforms Regions	Become naturalists/ campers and plan a camping trip Become a zoologist and design a habitat	Plan a camping trip including supplies and activities, camp out, invite parents and community members to participate; design a habitat or portion of a habitat and partner with local zoologist to present designs and model

Any Content	Become a game designer	Create board or digital games based on content, share with other students to learn the content Involve game designers, game companies, or graphic designers
States and Symbols or Countries Geography	Collaborate with a school, class, or group in another state, country, or region	Students research a state or country and share their findings with the other school, class, group
Rocks/ Earth Science Native Americans	Become archaeologists and museum curators	Create a museum with exhibits of Native American artifacts, rocks, fossils, invite parents and community members to tour the exhibits; involve local museum curators and experts, display exhibits in local museum or public libraries
Any Content	Become website developers/ bloggers	Create a website or blog to share information about a topic with the world, partner with bloggers, influencers, or web designers
Math/ Literacy/ Social Studies	Become an interior designer	Design your own classroom, library, or space; interview and work with actual clients, learn from interior designers and experts, have the experts and clients serve as the audience
Any Content	Become an app designer	Design an app that would solve a real-world problem, invite app designers to mentor students and judge final apps
Science/ Math/Health	Become a chef	Learn the essentials of cooking/ recipes/measurement and have an Iron Chef Cook-Off or Cupcake Challenge, invite real chefs to judge the competitions

BE REAL: AUTHENTICITY

Before we take the incredible idea you just married to the step-by-step planning phase, I would encourage you to do one more quick validity test. Will you please check your "what if?" project for authenticity? That might seem confusing, since we just worked through this whole process of brainstorming, including a real-world consideration step, but I have found that sometimes I get ahead of myself and lose authenticity.

Let me shed some light on my thinking. Our home always seemed to be the place where our kids' friends hung out. This made for a chaotic, but fun, place to be!

On one typical Friday evening toward the end of the school year, a gaggle of girls was hovering in my kitchen eating handfuls of M&M's, Cheetos, and Oreos while I cooked up a batch of pasta for dinner. They were chattering and giggling about everything from prom to graduation. One of the girls griped about all the homework being assigned and one particular project that was "just so stupid." After listening to the whining for a while, I had to ask what in the world had the teacher assigned that was just so stupid. She said that they were assigned a travel brochure in her world geography class. A travel brochure? What is the big deal? I mean, I have assigned travel brochures. I have created travel brochures myself in class years ago. Why the hostility toward them?

I pressed for more information. "So what is the problem with making a travel brochure? You are really creative." She hit me with a response that stays with me forever: "Who uses travel brochures anymore?" This very smart young lady went on to say that no one plans a vacation or learns about a place looking at travel brochures these days. Everyone goes online and looks at blogs, websites, and social media for information. And you know what? She was right! She was not motivated to do the assignment because the task was inauthentic. I understand what the teacher was trying to accomplish and value her wanting to promote creativity, but the project was not authentic, and the high school students saw right through it.

Remember when I asked you to take off your teacher hat? It is not our fault—we live in an education bubble and sometimes hold on to things that have always been done in classrooms, even if they are a bit antiquated. There may still be a time and place for students to create travel brochures, but is that the only way they can show their understanding of a location? I encourage myself, and all of us, to double check for authenticity the products, presentations, and processes we have in mind for our PBL units. Does the project, product, process, or presentation really mirror the real world? Have we asked our students what the most authentic way to show the learning is?

One of my favorite recent commercials is for Esurance car insurance. It shows an older lady explaining to her friends how to post photos to her wall, her actual wall, and goes on to "defriend" her pal when she disagrees with her about car insurance prices. The defriended pal keeps saying "That's not how it works! That's not how any of this works." Cracks me up every time I watch it. Seems to me we do this all the time in school. We ask students to do assignments and projects that we have used for years and the kids are thinking or saying, "That is not how it works!" Let's be sensitive to this and try our best to move with the times. It isn't always possible, but at least we can try to have students do things the way they really work.

FORMULATING ESSENTIAL OR DRIVING QUESTIONS: MOVING FROM BRAINSTORMING TO UNIT PLANNING

We have our PBL unit "what if?"; we have checked for authenticity; and now we need to construct our essential question so we can move to putting the pieces into our unit plan. What is an essential, or driving, question? The essential or driving question serves as the road sign that helps us get where we want to go in the unit. Each time the students, or we, want to add an idea or change course, we look to the essential question to remind us of our focus, which keeps us back track.

It's tempting to overcomplicate an essential question. We like to add teacher jargon and make it sound "smart." Fight the urge of wordiness. Here are four key things to keep in mind when writing essential questions.

- The essential question should be student friendly. Students should understand the question and the purpose of the PBL unit.
- The essential question should be engaging and capture the interest of the students.
- The essential question should be open-ended and not something you can just google.
- The essential question should reflect the standards/purpose of the unit.

I recently noticed a thread on Twitter of PBL-ers discussing their essential questions. Take a look at these examples and consider if they address the four characteristics we just discussed:

- How do we recognize and celebrate community heroes?
- What materials can we use to make our playground safer?
- How can we, as stewards of the ocean, advocate for the protection of sharks?
- How can we improve the traffic flow in our community?
- How can our school best support our overall health and wellness?
- How can we publish our own texts inspired by our favorite authors?
- Do social media influencers have ethical responsibilities to society?

Using the characteristics and examples discussed, take time to write your essential or driving question. Provide a road sign for the learning ahead!

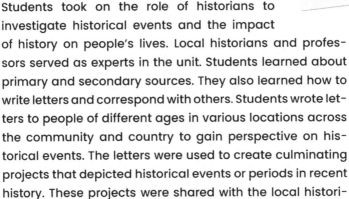

Essential Question: How can we, as historians, use letter writing to capture the stories of the past?

Content Areas: Writing, Social Studies

Students took on the role of historians to investigate historical events and the impact of history on people's lives. Local historians and professors served as experts in the unit. Students learned about primary and secondary sources. They also learned how to write letters and correspond with others. Students wrote letters to people of different ages in various locations across the community and country to gain perspective on historical events. The letters were used to create culminating projects that depicted historical events or periods in recent history. These projects were shared with the local historians, professors, school, and local community members.

PBL UNIT PLANNING: PUTTING PIECES TOGETHER STEP BY STEP

We are rolling now! Brainstorming is complete! You have your standards, project idea, "what if?" project, and essential question. It is time to take your thoughts and put them into actual plans. Take time to think through the entire unit from start to finish. How will you launch your PBL unit? What mini-lessons do you anticipate teaching? Now is the time to take the big idea and make it real. I like to use the planning sheets on pages 62 and 63:

PBL PLANNING: STEP BY STEP

Step One: Project Launch

> How will you launch the project?

Step Two: Challenge & Essential Question

> What is your essential question?

Step Three: Questions/Need to Know/Need to Do Chart

> You will create the chart with students after your launch. Do you have any questions you want to add to the chart?

Step Four: Mini-Lesson/Modeling

> What mini-lessons do you anticipate teaching throughout the unit?

Step Five: Research

> What resources will you provide for research?

Step Six: Students Work & Teacher Confers with Students

> What types of products do you think students may create? What mini-lessons and examples will you need to model?

Step Seven: Prep & Rehearsal

> When do you anticipate being
> ready for prep and rehearsal?
> What might that look like?

Step Eight: Big Event/Sharing with a Real Audience

> When would you like to share the
> work with a public audience? What
> might you need for this final event?

Step Nine: Reflection

> How will you have students reflect?
> What will the final assessment be?

ASSESSMENT TIMELINE

In addition to the step-by-step plan, you will need an assessment timeline for the unit. We want to build in assessment throughout the weeks of learning and working on the project. We will discuss more about assessment in chapter 6, but begin thinking about how you want to assess the learning during your unit.

How are you feeling about lesson planning for PBL now? Are you comfortable with the planning process? I want you to make planning your own, but I also want you to feel equipped with a strategy to get you started. I want to share one last tool to help you as you are finishing your PBL unit plans. This is a simple self-reflection that incorporates the key elements and principles of PBL. I use it to make sure I am including all that is needed to have a robust and rigorous PBL unit. We are doing our best to avoid fluff-and-stuff, so tools like this keep me on point.

	SELF-REFLECTION: PBL UNIT PLANNING	
✓	MUST-HAVES	THOUGHTS/QUESTIONS
	My project is based on important standards or cluster of standards.	
	I have written an Essential Question that is student friendly.	
	My project is real-world and students will have an authentic role or challenge.	
	I know what to assess, when to assess, and how. I have my assessment timeline created.	
	Students will have choice and voice. I have included students in decision making throughout the project.	
	Students will learn as we work on the project, not just submit something at the end of the unit.	
	I will kick off the unit with a hook that gets everyone pumped about learning.	
	Students will be doing the work! They will be researching, planning, and creating.	
	I have built in mini-lessons and modeling to scaffold the learning.	
	I have planned for ongoing conferencing and will check in with students daily.	
	We have a public audience who appreciates the work.	
	I have created a project timeline and set deadlines.	

The final step in planning a PBL unit is to take the overall plans and sit with our calendar for a few moments. Schedule deadlines and break the unit into manageable daily chunks. There is some guesswork here because we don't know exactly how long things will take and students will work at different paces, but we can generalize where we would like to be within the time frame selected. It might look something like this:

Week	MONDAY	TUESDAY	WEDNESDAY	THURSDAY	FRIDAY
1	Project Launch	Challenge/ Essential Question Chart: Questions/ Need-to-Knows/ Need-to-Dos	Mini-Lesson	Mini-Lesson	Begin Research
2	Research/ Conferring	Research/ Conferring	Mini-Lesson	Mini-Lesson	Product Planning/ Creation Conferring
3	Product Planning/ Creation Conferring	Product Planning/ Creation Conferring	Product Planning/ Creation Conferring	Mini-Lesson	Product Planning/ Creation Conferring
4	Mini-Lesson	Finalizing Products/ Presentations	Finalizing Products/ Presentations	Prep and Rehearsal	Prep and Rehearsal
5	Prep and Rehearsal	Public Audience	Reflection	Final Assessment	

Well, there you have it! From brainstorming to daily lesson plans, you have taken a big idea for a project and made it doable. I am excited to celebrate your successes! I would love to hear from you! Share your PBL ideas, successes, and struggles at #PBLanywhere and visit drlorielliott.com for more resources and opportunities to collaborate!

LIVE IT! LEARN IT! LOVE IT!

- Brainstorm PBL unit ideas by focusing on standards, what the standards look like in the real world, "what if" project ideas, and resources available.

- Check PBL project ideas for authenticity.

- Move from brainstorming to the step-by-step plan to visualize the entire PBL unit.

- Establish daily and weekly plans for the PBL unit after establishing all the steps.

- PBL Goes Virtual: Consider your technology tools and resources. Try to use the tools your students are already familiar with during the PBL unit if possible.

REVISITING RESEARCH IN THE CLASSROOM

A few years ago, while serving as a technology integration specialist, I was asked by a colleague to assist her with a seventh-grade research project about the Middle Ages. She would get the research started, and I would assist the students with creating blogs, websites, podcasts, and other fun endeavors. So, when the project started, I grabbed my laptop and headed to the computer lab to observe the first day of the research-project work. Very quickly I saw that both the teacher and students were already frustrated by the experience. Some students were clear about the purpose of the project and were searching websites and taking notes. Others were unsure and copying everything on the screen. A few students had already jumped into creating a website, neglecting fact finding all together, and a small group of boys was fixated on a video game they had come across when "researching." Needless to say, the teacher had to reboot the whole research process. What happened? Why were the middle schoolers so lost?

In this chapter we are going to revisit research in the classroom. We are going to discuss important principles for starting, doing, and sharing research. We are examining this from the perspective of PBL, but the ideas can be used for any type of research projects.

Think about the following questions.

- What do you immediately think of when I say the word research?
- What does research look like in the classroom?

Thank you for pondering this with me. When I ask teachers around the country to consider these questions, I typically get the following types of responses:

- Research is reading books and online resources and taking notes.
- Research is googling information.
- I see students working on computers during research.
- I see lots of books and notes during research.
- I see graphic organizers and students writing research papers.
- I see students typing reports and research papers.

These responses are not wrong, but I would like to expand our view of research as it pertains to PBL. I believe research is much more than reading and writing notes. I am going to try and convince you with some familiar examples from television. This may seem like a stretch, but I think they are a very practical way to view research.

Bazinga!

Are you a fan of the popular comedy *The Big Bang Theory*? You know . . . Leonard, Penny, Sheldon, and all the gang? In this sitcom, most of the main characters are scientists. We have watched these lovable geeks involved in various research projects through the years. What have we observed them doing while conducting research? When we think of scientific research, we visualize experiments and whiteboards filled with formulas. We see test tubes, chemicals, and explosions.

In fact, if you google "research," the first definition will be similar to this: "the systematic investigation into and study of materials and sources in order to establish facts and reach new conclusions." Scroll down from the definitions for research and notice all the links to research studies. My point is that research very often has an investigation component. We seek to discover answers by trial and error. Research in PBL may involve experiments and case studies. So, grab the beakers and get students to access their inner Sheldon. Bazinga!

What a Way to Start the Day!

The *Today Show* or *Good Morning America*? You may not have much time to watch morning TV, but I am sure you are familiar with some of the morning crew personalities. Whether you watch Savannah, Hoda, Craig, Robin, Michael, or George with your cup of joe, you observe research in action.

Each of these morning hosts shows us another side of research. How do they get the scoop on the latest news and Hollywood buzz? That's right: they ask questions of guests and experts. It may also be true they have their assistants and interns collect information, but they spend their mornings interviewing people about various topics and events.

What can we learn from our morning friends? PBL research often involves asking experts questions and learning from their responses. Interviews, surveys, and conversations are important ways to research a topic. Going straight to the source is an authentic way to discover information. Just like the morning talk shows . . . PBL is the time for lights, camera, action also!

Be a Joanna!

I have already made reference earlier in our discussion to one of the most popular DIY shows ever, *Fixer Upper*. In my neck of the woods, Joanna and Chip Gaines are considered some kind of royalty. I am so not kidding. People in the Ozarks love the down-to-earth Texans that transform a run-down ranch-style house into a shiplapped, barn-door-filled mansion. I have found myself more than once binging on the popular show while sipping hot tea from my very own Magnolia mug.

I also see research in a new light when I consider the talent and creativity of Joanna Gaines. I believe she is constantly involved in research. She interviews couples and determines their style, needs, and likes in regard to home ownership. She then scours the countryside to find the right colors, materials, furniture, and décor to make the new house a home. She studies pictures and swatches of paint colors and fabric. She examines wood grain, texture, and patterns. Joanna uses her senses to make the right choices.

Project-based learning may require students to explore many options, materials, and choices. They may need to analyze photographs, artwork, videos, or actual objects to understand concepts. Their senses may be engaged as they seek to learn. They also may have to tear down some unnecessary ideas or solutions. PBL may in fact be much like *Fixer Upper*: dream like Joanna and demo like Chip!

These three examples all point to a common theme. Research is bigger than just reading information and taking notes. Research can be experiments, simulations, interviews, surveys, experts, analyzing options, and listening to others. I would like to redefine research as simply "gathering information."

When I change my definition of research to gathering information, I recognize that I don't have to rely solely on books and online resources. There is absolutely a need to seek out high-quality information online and in published works, but examining pictures and talking with experts are also valid research strategies.

CONSIDER THE SOURCE

One of the biggest concerns about doing research in the classroom is the lack of resources and materials. You may have limited technology in your school or an ancient library. Maybe your students are working on research at home during virtual learning and they don't know where to begin. I understand your frustration. We never seem to have what we need in order to do what needs to be done. Before you panic, please take a moment to glance over my suggestions for research materials. My shopping list for resources aligns with my view that research is gathering information.

- Pictures and videos
- Guest speakers and experts
- Experiences (lessons, experiments, simulations, field trips)
- Books and audio books

- Websites/apps
- Podcasts

What do you notice about this shopping list? There is definitely a variety. Some of the resources are what we expect, and a few are a little outside the box. Your next question is probably, "And who is finding all this stuff? Because I don't have time to do one more thing." I hear you. We can barely keep our heads above water some days. Having said that, I will be honest that some, if not all, of the resource selection is done by the teacher. In many cases we are already locating resources, so we save time by intentionally searching for tools students can use during their own research. This may vary depending on the grade level you teach of course, but the teacher will always have to do some resource selection. Hang with me just a minute more while I make my case. I have three reasons I think it is important:

Content Curation

Content curation is the act of discovering, gathering, and presenting digital content that surrounds specific subject matter. Curation has become a trend in marketing and with online influencers. Individuals or companies sort through the vast expanse of online information and pull out or curate the best of the best for others to use. I found myself becoming a curator when I started my first teacher blog, Lori's Latest Links. I began the blog to help the teachers in my own school district quickly access helpful tech tools and information. I never thought about people outside my little community reading it, but they did! It was so much fun to find a gem that I enjoyed using with students and then share it with others. I was already looking for things for myself, I just took an extra minute and shared it online. Priceless!

Just as teachers benefited from my time and effort curating content for them, so do students. You see, I discovered the value of curating because of my classroom blogs. Prior to starting Lori's Latest Links, I used blogs in my classroom to help students navigate to the best online information, tools, videos, photos, and sites. I found that it saved time, helped students to focus, modeled selection of reliable sources, and scaffolded the research process.

Author John Spencer discusses curation on his amazing blog (spencerauthor.com), writing, "Teachers are already curators. We piece together resources, research, and ideas as we develop lessons. We curate the content that we teach. This isn't anything new or groundbreaking. It's what happens when we find a great book or video and share it with our students."

Curation of content is authentic. We as consumers take advantage of curated content daily. If you have ever followed We Are Teachers or popular educational bloggers, then you have experienced the joy and ease of learning because of their work. Curating content for our students is not doing the work for them, it is helping them do their work efficiently.

Now that many of us are teaching virtually or in a hybrid situation, curation becomes even more important. We can curate and organize resources for our students to access using digital choice boards or a simple digital bookmarking site such as Symbaloo. This not only gives the students guidance but makes the learning more focused on our standards and goals.

Differentiating Learning

Every group of students is composed of different personalities, interests, abilities, and backgrounds. Trying to meet all the needs can be challenging if not overwhelming. Providing a variety of research resources can assist in addressing these differences. We recognize that some students will flourish by asking questions of experts. Other learners need to experience lessons, simulations, and experiments to solidify ideas. Yet another cadre of students will benefit from reading articles and viewing videos. Do you have early readers or students that need extra support in reading? Sharing multiple options for gathering information will both assist and engage these learners. Research is not a reading assessment. It is gathering information to analyze, apply, or create a response or product.

Time and Frustration Saver

I am being real with this third reason for teacher selection of sources: it is a time and frustration saver! What takes the teacher a few moments to collect and share will take students hours or days of instructional time. Unless the PBL unit is targeting research skills, I opt for providing resources so that we can get busy! Even high school students can spend literally hours surfing online for sites and information. These same students will copy and paste everything because they are unsure what they are actually seeking in this process.

You guessed it—this leads to frustration for the students and the teacher. Without some scaffolding everyone can become easily frustrated. Why not take the resources you found when preparing for the unit and make them available to students? Add links to your Google Classroom account. Have the librarian pull the books you need. Bookmark YouTube videos. Email the guest speaker. Plan the experiment. You were already going to use those resources anyway. Save time in the unit by sharing.

Essential Question: What should a classroom look like so students can work and learn best?

Content Areas: Math and Social Studies

Students became designers to create ultimate learning environments for teacher clients. Students learned from interior decorators and architects about the design process. The students interviewed the teacher client and designed new classrooms to meet the needs of the individual teacher. Students created sketches, models, and presentations to share with the teacher client. The students developed measurement, budgeting, and map skills throughout the project.

MIDDLE SCHOOL - PBL UNIT -

Now that we have revisited research in the classroom, let's see what it might look like in different grade levels. What might this resource shopping list look like in classrooms? Here are a few examples:

Kindergarten

PBL Unit: How can we stay healthy in winter?
 Research materials:

- Videos from *PBS Kids*, *Sesame Street*, and Discovery Education
- Guest speakers: doctors and nurses
- Experiences: lessons about germs and handwashing
- Pictures of winter, appropriate clothing, healthy foods, and activities
- Books about winter and winter preparation
- Digital choice board for students to use while learning online that includes the selected links

High School

PBL Unit: How can urban farming improve communities?
 Research materials:

- Photos and videos from urban farming nonprofit organizations
- Online articles, websites, blogs
- Published reports
- Newspaper and television news stories
- Guest speakers: urban farming experts, community activists, community leaders, university professors, nonprofit directors
- Podcasts
- How-to books about urban farming
- Links posted on Google Classroom or another LMS platform for easy access

Seems doable? Chances are in preparing for our PBL units, we will find most of the resources while educating ourselves about the topics included in our units.

> This was the year I think I grew the most. I came in very shy and reserved and left as a "social butterfly." So many hands-on, group projects helped me use my voice and learn to work with others. And if you didn't do your research you were letting down your group!
>
> —Kristie Ballard Uttinger

ReSearch Without Tears

Consider this: having the right tools in your toolbox does not necessarily mean you will be able to build the birdhouse. Even when we provide the most appropriate research resources and materials, we don't ensure research is going to happen. Students need to know the process of researching. Let's teach them to build the birdhouse! Here are some tips for actually doing the research.

Model, Model, Model

Show and Tell is not just for kindergarten. We must model the steps of the research process by showing how to tackle each aspect of this complicated endeavor. Use your mini-lessons at the beginning of the unit to show and tell how to use the resources, graphic organizer, paraphrasing, note-taking, citing, etc. Leave nothing to chance. Think through what it is like to stare at a computer or book, unsure what to do next. Consider how to construct questions for an expert. Ponder how you learn from an experiment and capture your learning by note-taking. Then show students how you do all these things!

I spend a lot of time collaborating with small groups of teachers to plan, reflect, and brainstorm PBL units. I love it! It truly is the most important work I am privileged to do. In a recent session, a group of high school teachers were frustrated to no end about the agonizing process of having students do research in their first unit. I listened to all the things the students did wrong, couldn't do, or wouldn't do. My response was to ask, "How did you model that with your students?" I heard things like, "I gave them examples." "I told them the requirements." "I told them to read the articles." With further discussion it became evident that there was little *show* and lots of *tell* in their "modeling." No judgement here. We have all done similar things. We assume that because of the age or grade level, students should know how to do this already. Unfortunately, it doesn't usually work that way.

Students need to watch us in action and hear what our brain is saying as we work. For example, one weakness for many students is the ability to read online and paraphrase. The amount of text on the screen overwhelms some students and they check out. To help them deal with this, I project a website on the large screen and think aloud how I would tackle it. I literally say things like, "Good grief, there are too many words on this screen. Ugh! Let me cover part of this so I can make sense of this. OK, now I get it. Let me move this paper covering the text and look at the next paragraph. What is it telling me? It says that recycling water bottles can be expensive, and they are taking up so much space in landfills. We need to just use our own reusable cups and quit wasting resources."

You get it. Show and Tell . . . Model research practices and strategies at the beginning of the unit to get students moving and throughout the research phase as needed.

Graphic Organizers, Sketchnotes, and More
Students need a way to internalize the information gathered during research. We tell students to take notes, but I have found most don't really understand what that means. I will look over and see students writing down everything from the source because they aren't sure what is important.

I would like to suggest that we provide choice in note-taking. The use of *graphic organizers* is a great starting point. After we have established the chart questions/need-to-knows/need-to-dos we can create simple graphic organizers that help students answer the questions and find the need-to-knows. It might be a simple chart like the following examples:

URBAN FARMING	
What is urban farming?	How is urban farming affecting communities?
What are the disadvantages to urban farming?	Resources needed for urban farming

Sketchnoting is another highly effective method of note-taking. Author and educational consultant Sylvia Duckworth popularized sketchnoting for the classroom. She describes sketchnoting as "a form of visual-notetaking. You draw or doodle your thoughts, observations, or notes in combination with words or text. Sketchnoting is *not* art. It is a very personal way to document your thought process."

Today's learners are very visual, and providing them with the option of taking notes visually is very appealing to them. I have found students to be very responsive to this method. Again, we model how to take sketchnotes and show many examples. I admit freely that I am not an artist, but this isn't about artwork. It is about our personal connection to the content.

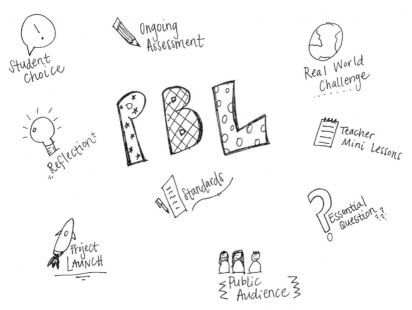

Sketchnote by Ashlyn Elliott

77

Our primary challenge with note-taking is helping students paraphrase the information in their own words. Paraphrasing differs from summarizing. Paraphrase is to express the meaning of the information presented, whether in writing or spoken, using different words, especially to achieve greater clarity. Summarizing means to construct a brief statement of the main points presented.

I have found that the most helpful way to model paraphrasing is to use the tried and true: I Do, We Do, You Do method of instruction. I use a written piece of text and talk aloud as I write my paraphrase of the content in front of the students. Then I provide partners or small groups a text for them to paraphrase. We discuss the results. Finally, students try it on their own with their research topics. As I confer with students through the unit, I can check in on their paraphrasing and note-taking.

Let's Give 'Em Something to Talk About

One simple way to check for understanding and build motivation for research is to provide opportunities for students to talk about their findings with other students. When we discuss our topic with other people, we realize how much we know or don't know. We get great questions from our listener and we are intrinsically motivated to dig for more dirt! This doesn't have to take up tons of time or be a huge thing, but it is extremely valuable.

Consider one of these Talk About It ideas:

- Partner Share: Take a few moments at the end of a research period or work time and ask students to partner with another student to share what they discovered in their own words.
- Play Two Facts and a Fib: Each student shares three statements about their research. Two are true facts and one is a fib or misinformation. The partner guesses and the students discuss the results.
- Padlet or Jamboard: Use a tech tool such as Padlet or Jamboard to have students share the key findings in their research with classmates.

- Walk and Talk: At the beginning of class, put on some music and get students up and walking around the room with a partner. Have them discuss their research findings until the music stops. When the music stops, they change partners. This only needs to take a few minutes, but it solidifies the learning and helps students discover other questions they want to answer.
- Circle Up: Have everyone stand in a circle and have each student briefly share one thing they have learned from researching.

Put Research into Action

The purpose of doing the research in our units is to put the information into action. Students will be writing, designing, creating, building, or producing something to demonstrate their application of the information. The research in PBL is fuel to our fire! It propels us to action. It allows us to understand the world better and make change. It is easy to get caught in the web of research and forget our why.

Guide students to take what they now know and do something with it. If students see the information as separate or unconnected, they will not produce an outcome that is authentic and worthy of the challenge. Look at what can happen if we don't help students connect the research with action:

Ms. Awesome Teacher challenges her students to find something in the community that needs to be improved or changed to make the community better. The students distribute surveys, research the services and programs available within the small town, and interview community leaders. However, after all the research is completed, the students want to pursue having a skate park built in the local park because it would be "so much fun." The research doesn't show this as a need or even a want in the town.

Houston, we have a problem! The research should be connected to the project and be the why for the work done within the unit. Ms. Awesome Teacher will need to redirect her students and hold them accountable to the research to decide on a solution for the community. Just as we are constantly being reminded as teachers to know our why . . . students need to know their why also in their PBL work!

Middle school students were challenged to design their dream house and then determine how many lights would be needed to decorate the home for the holidays. Students learned about slope and calculated the cost and amount of lights needed. They shared their dream homes and presentations with community members.

We started by switching our mindset about research from sitting and getting information out of an encyclopedia to putting research findings into action in our units. Take a moment to reflect on the following questions:

- How have you tackled research with your students in the past?
- What, if any, resources did you provide?
- How do you feel about doing some prep work ahead of the unit to locate a variety of quality sites, sources, and experiences?
- Do you think it is necessary?

The best thing I can tell you about doing research with students is to take it in small chunks and be very intentional about the resources, process, and outcomes.

LIVE IT! LEARN IT! LOVE IT!

- Research is gathering information. Consider the following research resources:
  - Pictures and videos
  - Guest speakers and experts
  - Experiences (lessons, experiments, simulations, field trips)
  - Books and audio books
  - Websites/apps
  - Podcasts
  - Provide graphic organizers, modeling, and scaffolding for researching topics.
  - Confer with students while they research to answer questions and guide the process.

- PBL Goes Virtual: Use digital choice boards or technology bookmarking tools like Symbaloo to organize resources for students. Favorite ed tech leaders such as Kasey Bell and Matt Miller provide helpful guides to using digital choice boards with students.

FLY-BYS, SIT DOWNS, AND OTHER ADVENTURES IN CONFERRING

I don't know about you, but I learn the most through failure. It is not something I enjoy or seek, but when it happens—and it has happened a lot—I take notice and change my ways. Such is the case with understanding the importance of conferring. I learned my lesson and I hope I can help you avoid my mistakes.

Let me set the scene. Back in the day, my students and I were deeply disturbed by news reports about the destruction of the Amazon rain forest. The idea of glorious trees being cut down, the dangers of the greenhouse effect, and the displacement of exotic animals was, and still is, so tragic. My young scientists were motivated into action! I used this desire to help the world as an emotional hook for our rain forest PBL unit. I kicked things off by showing pictures and video clips of the beautiful Amazon region, the glorious canopy, the adorable sloths, and the plight facing the region. I had a guest speaker share their experience of visiting the Amazon River.

We discussed what we knew about the urgent situation and made lists of questions we had, things we wanted to learn, and our ideas for saving the rain forest. The students worked in groups to research various animals and plants living in this lush habitat. They decided to learn all they could about the ecosystem, create their own life-size rainforest, and give tours of the habitat to educate others about the situation. They would also (as a class) collect donations for a non-profit organization working toward saving the Amazon rainforests. At this stage in the story, everything is roses and sunshine! Students are excited about learning and I am feeling like teaching is definitely my calling.

In the midst of all this bliss, I got caught up in the momentum and left learning to chance. You see, I didn't take time to sit with the groups of students and really investigate what they were doing. I was so pleased to see the students excited and busy that I assumed we were deepening our understanding of the rain forest and how to save it. I zipped around the room while students were working. It looked like everyone was engaged. I saw books, notes, butcher paper, scissors, poster board, markers everywhere. I mean, those are clear signs of meeting the curriculum, right? Class period after class period, I continued making circles around the room asking if anyone needed anything. I kept getting the thumbs up, so I kept moving.

After almost a week and a half, I decided to slow my roll and sit with each little group for a status check of where they were and what they were actually doing. You know where this story is headed, right?

My Pinterest-perfect teaching tale is about ready to meet reality. I sat down with one group of students who were super jazzed about their plans for the rain forest creation, but they had no research accomplished. They made yards of green vines out of butcher paper, but not a stitch of research was presented to support their topic. I sent them back to square one and insisted they show me some notes about their topic. Another group came to see me. I asked them to tell me what they were learning and where they were in the process. One young man proudly spoke up. "I am learning a lot about polar bears!" Yes, you heard right. Polar bears. I know I looked confused, and the other members of his group stared at me with that "Now you know what we have been dealing with" face. I asked him why he was focusing on the polar bears when we were trying to save the rain forest. No lie, he said . . . "We are? I just thought we were learning about animals."

As I continued meeting with each group, I found some groups were on top of things, but many were on their own paths far from our goal. How could I have missed this? Two weeks in and I had students focusing on the wrong habitat and continent! We were busy, excited, and looked like we were learning, but the students were all over the place, and we weren't hitting our target standards. In that moment of panic, my first reaction was very adultlike . . . blame the kids! It was their fault. They should have listened. They should have known better. But alas, it was my fault. I learned through that experience, the power of the conference. I missed everything because I had not utilized conferring correctly.

POWER OF THE CONFERENCE

Without scheduled and intentional conferences, our PBL units can quickly spin out of control. Without purposeful conferring we end up with low-quality products, superficial understanding of our standards, and sometimes no work completed at all.

Have you ever experienced something similar when working on a PBL unit or a project? If you have ever been frustrated by the quality of work or the lack of effort put forth, reflect on your conferring. How often did you meet with students? Did you meet with all students, even the "good" ones? I find that my approach to conferring in a unit is truly the make-or-break in having a successful unit. So how do we meet with so many students over the course of a unit? What do we say? What is the purpose? How do I do this virtually? Stick with me as I outline my approach to conferring. It helped me not only get all my students back where they needed to be in the rainforest, but it has guided my PBL work all these years. Learn from my mistakes!

Essential Question: Is organic produce worth the cost?

Content Area: Science

HIGH SCHOOL - PBL UNIT -

> Students were challenged with determining if organic produce was healthier and cost effective. Over the course of several months, the students investigated organic gardening compared with traditional gardening methods. They worked with expert gardeners and agriculture specialists to plant outdoor garden beds and hydroponic garden systems. They compared the soil and produce of each type of garden. They documented their progress and results. They shared their findings with the experts and community members during a school-wide exhibition night.

Fly-By Conferences

Each of my PBL units typically have three type of conferences: fly-bys, sit-downs, and student-requested. These conferences take place at different points in the journey, but all are important. Fly-bys are the most common type of conferences in classrooms. As students are working, we fly by students to check on them, answer questions, and redirect behavior. This type of conference has its place. Students need to have accountability, and knowing the teacher is moving around the room provides a level of responsibility. Teachers can answer questions as students are working and clarify concepts as we see misunderstandings. We can also encourage students as they work and listen to their thinking. These conferences are informal and can keep students on their toes.

However, when we only do fly-by conferences, we can also miss things. We tend to fly by where the trouble seems to be, so we often unintentionally skip over the well-behaved student because they seem to have it all together. They look like they are doing the right thing, so we keep moving. We tend to also ask simple questions when zipping by like, "Everything going OK? Do you need anything? Do you have any questions for me?" It is easy for students to respond positively and we accept their responses and continue to fly. Again, we miss what is actually happening. Students are Oscar-worthy actors. They can scam us.

I use fly-by conferences in the first few days of a PBL unit as students are starting their research. I also tend to revert to fly-bys in the very last days of a unit, when we are putting the final touches on a project. As an example, a middle school science class is exploring the question, "What is the best learning environment for middle school students to be successful?" Students are researching ideas such as sleep, nutrition, attention span, temperature, etc., that should be considered when creating middle school scheduling and learning environments. Once the unit is launched, mini-lessons have begun and the students are in groups digging into the topics, it would be wise to use the fly-by strategy. The teacher moves around the room and checks in with students to help them use the resource materials and technology correctly, focus on graphic organizers provided, and checking understanding of the content. It would also be appropriate at the end of the unit to reinstate fly-bys when students are completing their presentations and products to share with the school-district leadership team about their proposals for middle school scheduling and classrooms.

Those of us teaching virtually will quickly recognize that fly-bys are not as easy to accomplish in this setting. We can use our videoconferencing tools to informally check in with students as they work through a PBL unit. We might ask students to submit a daily video using Seesaw or Flipgrid to explain the work they are completing at each stage of the unit.

Sit-Down Conferences

Formal conferences, or sit-downs, are used during the majority of work days during my PBL units. Throughout a class period of work time I try to sit down with each group and have a targeted discussion about their learning and progress in the unit. If students are working independently, I still put groups of students together for these conferences to save time.

What do we discuss? One of the most helpful tools I have created for myself is a unit conference record sheet. This will vary based on my project, but it looks like this:

Student Name	Understands the Essential Question	Topic Selection	Research	Planning of Product/ Presentation	Creation of Product/ Presentation	Prep & Rehearsal	Public Audience	Reflection

I want to see the whole picture of the where we are as we are working, so I list all the students' names on my conference sheet. I then label each step in the project across the top. I customize this based on what we, as a class, decide we want to accomplish in the unit. I usually make my conference sheet after we chart the questions/need-to-knows/need-to-dos chart on the second or third day of the unit.

After I do a day or two of fly-by conferences to get everyone going, I then begin meeting with groups using this sheet. Notice I always start with the essential question. I want to make sure each student really understands what we are doing and what the goal is for the unit. Then, I move to the next step in the process and ask students to show me their work. I ask in-depth questions and facilitate the learning based on their responses. After each quick conference, I make notes and check off the topic discussed. This provides me with a helpful guide for each conference. I don't rehash earlier conversations but start where my checkmarks and notes end.

Let's revisit our middle school example. After the initial day or two of research, the teacher begins calling each group of students to a table to check in during their sit-down conferences. The teacher uses a conference sheet outlining the steps in the project. The conference will only last a few moments but is very structured. It sounds something like this: *Hey, guys. How is it going? Yesterday when we met, you were showing me your research findings on your graphic organizer. You were finishing up your notes. Can I please see your notes? Are they finished? (Teacher reads the notes.) Awesome! You really have a good understanding of the facts. Looks like your group's next step is to determine the best solution for helping middle school students succeed based on your research. What is your plan to make this decision and how do you envision sharing this with the school-district leaders?"*

The teacher uses his/her notes to guide each day's discussion and help students set goals for the work ahead. Checking in briefly every day pinpoints trouble spots and helps the teacher to know what is needed and where everyone is in the process.

There was a time when I thought I could remember earlier discussions with students and where each group was in the process during a unit, but I gave that up years ago. I can't keep all that straight without some kind of simple note-taking. I adjust the size of spaces in my chart so I can take notes, or I keep an additional notebook of more anecdotal notes to correspond with my chart. This has truly been a game changer for me! Simply being intentional in scheduling daily conferences and making myself take notes raised the quality of learning and products to a higher level.

Sit-downs are used throughout the middle part of my PBL units. They are like the creamy filling of an Oreo cookie, if you will. They are put into use once everyone is up and running in the unit and behavior expectations are being met. They work well because students recognize that they will speak with the teacher daily, if only for a few short minutes. This creates structure and accountability for everyone. Students will come to expect these visits and a more open conversation tends to take place. Conferring builds community, and I want my students to see our classroom as a safe place where they can try, fail, question, celebrate, and succeed.

Sit-downs become Zoom-ins with students learning online. In other words, we schedule formal conversations with students or groups of students to see and talk with them about their work using videoconferencing. We want to do these synchronously so the discussion is fluid and we can provide feedback immediately.

Student-Requested

Even with fly-by and sit-down conferences in place, students may still have some questions or need individual help. I let students know that they can be proactive and request a conference if they need help with something that they feel would be better discussed individually. I have typically used Post-It Notes. Students put their name on a Post-It Note and add it to our chart of questions/need-to-knows/need-to-dos. When taking PBL virtual, use a site like Padlet or Jamboard so students can add digital sticky notes to a digital wall/board you create for the project. When I see these, I work with the student to find a time to meet.

This may be within the class period or before/after school. Not all students will take advantage of this type of conference, but I like to make them aware of the option. I know some teachers rely a great deal on student-requested conferences, but I choose to use this as an additional option because I know way too many students who will never schedule a conference.

Essential Question: How can we use the arts to inspire our community?

Content Area: Fine Arts

A fine-arts teacher challenged students to develop some way of sharing their love for the arts with their community. The students surveyed classmates, family members, and community members regarding needs and appreciation of the fine arts. Students worked together to create a fine arts night that would spotlight all the various types of art being created by the students. A musical concert, fashion show, art and photo gallery, and pottery demonstration were included in the fine arts night. Students, community members, local artists, and administration members attended the event.

FEEDBACK AND CONFERRING

"Mom, what was your favorite part?" I have been asked this question by my daughter, Ashlyn, more times than I can count. Ashlyn taught me the importance of feedback and how to give effective feedback. She has been singing, dancing, and acting on stage since she was in second grade. From the *Three Piggy Opera* to *Little Shop of Horrors* to *Sunday in the Park with George*, I've been there for every scene and curtain call.

When we first started attending Ashlyn's dance recitals, choir concerts, and musicals, I would shower her with a bouquet of flowers and compliments after the performance. Every single time she would accept the compliment with a thank you, but I could tell in her scrunched-up face she wanted more. She would follow up immediately, "But what was your favorite part?"

I quickly learned that I was not going to get by with generic praises. Ashlyn wanted true feedback. She wanted to know specifically which scene, song, dance move, etc., was impressive. She wanted my thoughts on how to make it better the next time. I started taking notes during performances so I would have specific examples to reference in our after-show conferences. I am kidding, sort of.

You see, I really did learn from Ashlyn that words matter. Providing encouragement and specific feedback makes a big difference in getting results in the future. I also learned I must have an excellent relationship with the person I am providing feedback to. If, for some reason, Ashlyn's performance was not up to her standards, I knew to tread lightly because she was already reflective and being hard on herself. I would choose to emphasize the specific areas of strength and for the time being, let her sort out the weaknesses. These interactions with my daughter helped me learn to provide effective feedback to my students.

Conferences provide us a systematic way to share feedback with students. We listen to what they say and guide their thinking with questions and targeted comments. Feedback is more than just a pat on the back or another "Good job!" Pat Sachse-Brown and Joanne Aldridge explain the importance of good feedback this way: "Effective feedback is about finding the best way of communicating to learners what they have achieved and what they need to work on next." Effective feedback provides students with guidance to help them succeed. This feedback is descriptive and should provide specific information related to a target goal. It should be immediate or timely. And this is why conferring is so very important; it allows us to provide descriptive feedback about the work the students are doing in real time, and it is specific to our learning targets within the PBL unit. Such great teaching!

One strategy I find useful in providing feedback while conferring with students is this simple concept:

WHAT'S WORKING?	WHAT'S NOT?	WHAT'S NEXT?

In her discussion of the purpose of feedback, educator and author Jan Chappuis shares a reflective question we should ask when conferring or giving feedback to students: "Can this student take action on this comment?" Effective feedback is actionable. This simple organizer reminds me to assist students in taking the next steps in their work.

LIVE IT! LEARN IT! LOVE IT!

- Conferring with students is the key to a successful PBL unit. Conducting consistent and positive conferences with students raises the quality of a project.

- Use fly-by conferences to get students started in the unit and at the end to help pull things together.

- Use sit-down conferences throughout most of the unit to have more in-depth discussions.

- Provide opportunity for students to request additional conferences.

- Use a note-taking system such as a chart, Post-It Notes, spreadsheet, app, or a notebook to keep a record of discussions and goals for each student.

- Listen more than talk. Listen to the students to guide your conversations.

- Make conferences a regular part of your PBL experience to develop accountability.

- Build relationships and community through your conferences. Focus on the learner first, not the content.

- PBL Goes Virtual: Use scheduled synchronous conferences throughout a PBL unit and asynchronous tools such as Seesaw, Flipgrid, Padlet, and Jamboard to check in with students while they are working.

ASSESSMENT AND AUDIENCE: KEYS TO AUTHENTICITY AND ACCOUNTABILITY

love sharing my passion for PBL with educators. I watch during my workshops for the moment when PBL starts to really make sense. I see wrinkled brows and uptight shoulders start to ease. I listen to the energetic conversations that start bubbling with ideas about saving the world, helping the community, and making learning meaningful for students. I anticipate that in the eventual deeper discussions, teachers will start asking about assessment. I celebrate those questions because we should be asking about how to assess the learning done during PBL. Assessment is not negative, but rather a vital process in our PBL success. So if you have been pushing aside questions about assessment and grading because you thought it would cloud the joy of project-based learning, have no fear! Assessment is another important element in the PBL must-haves.

Let's do a little clarification about the purpose of assessment in our PBL units. Assessment is not just putting grades in the grade book, although it will help us with grading. Assessment is not a hoop to jump through to show our administrators that we are doing our job, yet we are indeed being amazing employees. Assessment is not to keep parents off our backs, even though it will ease concerns for some. Assessment does not mean stacks of papers to grade; in fact, we will use organic forms of assessment that will ease our workload. Assessment, when done authentically, will help us guide our students and better facilitate learning.

I know that at the end of the day, even with all the power of PBL in your classroom, you still have to give grades. There is a quiet nagging in your ear, constantly reminding you that we are responsible for standardized assessments, grades, and progress reports. I see you and I hear you! We can do PBL right and fulfill all those needs.

GROUP GRADES OR NOT?

Are you like me and always a little tempted to take the newest personality test on BuzzFeed that pops up on your social media feed? You know the type: "What Muppet are You Most Like?" or "Which Character on *Friends* are You?" I've not only been tempted; I've taken more than one of those quizzes in recent years. The results are in and I am most definitely like Miss Piggy and Rachel. Try to make sense of that data. I know. Mind blowing.

I bring this up because we are all unique and approach tasks differently. Some of us are independent and like to take control of situations and just "get 'er done!" Others tend to observe and process things before acting. Some people prefer directions and step-by-step guidance to make sure they are doing it right. There are even a few of us who don't want to do anything and are pleased as punch to let everyone else do the heavy lifting. I am not judging, just stating the obvious. We have all seen this difference in personality and work ethic when working on a committee or a group project in school.

Group work, group projects, and cooperative learning are not new to education. We learned long ago that students can benefit from small-group work and develop communication, collaboration, critical thinking, and creativity skills when working with others. But just as we are all different Muppets or characters from *Friends*, students are unique and bring to group experiences their own baggage and strengths. Much of PBL is collaborative and takes place in small-group work. How do we assess student work? Group grades or not?

I am not a fan of group grades. I am not alone. Parents and students have a strong dislike of group grades also. The main complaint seems to be that group grades are just not fair. We know that some members of a group may work harder, know more, or sit by and let everyone else put forth all the effort. Well-respected educator and assessment expert Rick Wormeli states in his book *Fair Isn't Always Equal,* "Group grades don't reflect an individual student's achievement or growth and therefore can't be used to document progress, provide feedback, or inform instructional decisions regarding individual students." He continues, "For most group situations, however, students will experience the group project and receive ample descriptive feedback, but we will assess students outside of the group experience in order to see what individual students took away from that group experience." I wholeheartedly agree with this approach!

Instead of group grades, I want to know how each individual student is performing and learning during our units. I put practices into place that focus on the individual rather than the group, even though students may be working within a group for at least part of a project. I want to show you how to use formative and summative assessment tools that provide insight into the individual student's learning rather than relying on vague group grades that may not show a clear picture of what is really taking place.

ASSESSMENT OPTIONS

Not everyone enjoys shopping for clothes, but I do! It sounds cliché, but a little retail therapy every so often is good for my soul. Whether I am scrolling online for the perfect outfit or scouring the racks for a bargain, I love looking at all my options and selecting what works for me. At this stage in my life I have figured out the colors, styles, and sizes . . . ugh . . . that make me feel confident and comfortable.

Choices! Choices! We feel in control when we make choices. We are happier when given the opportunity to pick a solution rather than being mandated to do something. In the next few pages you will find a list of assessment options. I am going to ask you to select a few strategies to use in your next PBL unit. Don't feel you have to do them all. For those fashionistas out there, think of it like selecting an outfit. Grab the gorgeous top, pair it with a comfy pair of pants, and splurge on the necklace or tie. Choose three assessment tools that will work for your style and the goals of your upcoming unit. Ready to shop?

Essential Question: How can we save the bees?

Content Areas: Science, Communication Arts

The decline of bees in our environment impacts pollination and can potentially harm our food supply. The students learned about the contribution of bees in the ecosystem, the causes of bee disappearances, and solutions for saving the bees. Beekeepers and other experts were included in the project and served as part of the authentic audience. Students designed products and solutions for protecting and attracting bees to flowers and plants. They also developed educational materials to share with community members about the plight of the bees.

eLeMeNTARY
- PBL UNIT -

Teacher Observation Notes

Select a method for recording your observations and reflections during each day of the PBL unit. You may want to use a journal, notebook, or even sticky notes to jot down thoughts, questions, and observations during mini-lessons, work time, and discussions. You may want to document your notes using Google Docs or a favorite app. Whatever method you choose, recording your observations will help you informally assess how students are engaging with the content and process of the project.

Conference Notes/Charts

I am going to highly encourage you to keep conference notes through-out the project. We discussed conferring in depth earlier, and this serves as a reminder to use a conference sheet or chart to record notes. Conference notes will document the discussions, goals, and outcomes of each individual student. I like to use a conference chart for my con-ferring sessions. The chart outlines the steps in the PBL unit allowing me to clearly see where each student is within the stages of the project. I can jot down notes within the boxes or use this in addition to my teacher observation notes.

Learning Log/Project Notebooks or Journals

An excellent way to monitor individual growth during a unit is to have students keep a log/notebook/journal. I like calling these learning logs. Students can use a composition notebook, spiral notebook, etc., or they can keep track of things digitally using Seesaw or Google Docs. I do like using paper and pencil often because I want students to sketch and draw throughout the unit. The learning log is used for several things.

1. Plan and brainstorm
2. Show understanding of content and standards learned through-out the project
3. Design and make lists
4. Reflections
5. Goal setting for each day

I ask students to bring their learning log to our conferences so I can look at their progress and thinking. Learning logs are an authentic record of the work the students are doing. These can be scored if you need a daily or weekly grade.

Exit Slips and Formative Assessments

Many of us include exit slips as part of our instruction. Definitely incor-porate them during your PBL units. Because we are learning the stan-dards as students are working in the unit, exit slips allow you to check on the content/standards each week. For example, if your project is designing a home for veterans and you are focusing on the mathematical concepts of perimeter, area, square feet, etc., have students complete a problem for each of these standards on the exit slip and turn it in for you to check. These may or may not be scored for a grade, depending on your preference.

Checklists

There is something so satisfying about checking off things on a to-do list. Students find checklists helpful in seeing the big picture of a project, managing their time, and monitoring their own work. Once we have decided what our project will look like, I create my conference chart. Then I take those same steps and make a checklist for students to use so they can manage their work flow also.

	Essential Question and Challenge
	Research Topic Selected
	Research
	Plan for Product/Presentation
	Construction of Product/Presentation
	Feedback During Prep and Rehearsal
	Public Audience
	Reflection

Rubrics/Scoring Guides

I know you have been waiting for this one. We do need a rubric or scoring guide for the products and presentations students are accomplishing in our units. The rubric should include not only criteria for the product or presentation, and also how the standards or content was addressed in the final product/presentation. The students should be aware of the rubric early in the project, so they understand the expectations. It is also good practice to ask for student input when developing the rubric. This will likely take place after you complete your chart of questions/need-to-knows/need-to-dos. PBLWorks provides lots of helpful rubrics and scoring guides on their website. No need to create your own, use what they have already designed (https://www.pblworks.org).

Quizzes and Tests

Here are our familiar friends! My opinion on including quizzes and tests may go against others in the PBL world, but please hang in here with me and let me state my case. Some propose that we only use the rubric for the final product, as the main grade or assessment for a PBL unit. I can't justify that. I know the final result is important, but I want to see the whole picture, from the brainstorming through the process of working toward the culmination, and of course, the results. The bottom line is that most, if not all, students will be required to take a state or some type of standardized test at the end of the year or course. The benchmark and standardized tests required in a school, district, or state are not going away just because I am doing PBL. We aren't exempt from these types of assessments.

I want my students to not only learn at a deep level and create memories that last a lifetime because of our PBL units, but I want them to rock the traditional tests too! The only way they are going to do both is if I have shown them what they know in authentic ways as well as on a quiz or test. I give quizzes or checkpoints throughout the PBL unit that assess the standards we are learning during the unit, just as you give quizzes and checkpoints throughout a traditional chapter or unit of study. I also give a summative or unit test at the end of a PBL unit covering all the standards we were addressing during the unit. Again, just like you do when you give a unit or chapter test after weeks of traditional instruction. I like using engaging tech tools to assess student understanding of content such as Kahoot!, Quizizz, or Quizlet.

I do this so that students will see the content and skills presented in the same format that they will face on a standardized test. There is a bit of a game to taking standardized tests; it requires its own skill set. I have found that even when students know the content deeply because of our PBL unit and can authentically apply the information in real-world ways, they can stumble on a multiple-choice test or short-response question just because they don't know how to play the game of test taking.

Instead of doing drill-and-kill workbooks for assessment practice, I instead use the real-world learning we are doing in PBL and provide students with opportunities to express their understanding of the same content and standards they will face on traditional, standardized tests.

Trust me: this decision is the result of trial and error over the years. I explained early in the book that I embraced PBL from the start of my career. When testing, accountability, and test scores became the focus of the job of teaching, I had a tough decision to make. Do I abandon what I know is best for students or somehow learn to play the game? At first I was stubborn and held tightly to my version of PBL, which was focused on learning and reflections and not so much on the test scores. But once the spotlight was on state test scores, I realized quickly that my feelings and observations weren't going to satisfy the district's expectations for high scores. So I found a way to do both. We continued to do PBL, but I learned how to embed quizzes and tests throughout the unit to prepare my students for what was to come. At the same time, this actually gave me a better idea of what they were learning and what was still unclear to them.

My advice . . . play the game. You can do both! You can have authentic learning and student empowerment and high test scores. It takes intentionality and planning, but it is necessary and doable.

Written Reflections

Providing students with time to reflect during and after a PBL unit is so valuable. We have focused on the content and standards in many of the assessment tools shared so far. The written reflections should target the following things:

- Thoughts on their work
- Their understanding of concepts learned through the unit
- Thoughts on the final product or presentation
- Working with others
- Evaluating their time management or work flow
- How their work will impact others and make a difference
- What they would still like to learn more about

- Preferences for the next PBL unit

Student Plans and Task-Management Sheets

Even though these tools may not be for a grade, they can be used to guide students in developing time and task-management skills. They also provide us with more examples and information about why the students are succeeding or stumbling. Some students are overwhelmed with research or breaking a task into small parts. Using planning and management sheets can ease that anxiety and provide us with documentation to share with parents or the students themselves when discussing progress.

ASSESSMENT PLAN

When you begin planning your PBL units, think through when you will implement the assessment strategies you want to use. Plot out which assessment tools you would most like to employ and when you would like to integrate them within the unit. The reason I have found it essential to write this down is because if we don't, we forget. Life happens and we get caught up in the wave of activity.

Carefully consider how students will show what they know. Refer to your selected standards and think backward. Where do you want to end and where along the upcoming weeks will you place checkpoints and benchmarks? Your timeline might look something like this:

PBL UNIT: HOW CAN WE SAVE THE BEES? ASSESSMENT PLAN

TIMELINE	GOALS/STANDARDS	ASSESSMENTS	REFLECTIONS/ NOTES
Week One	Bee Vocabulary Pollination	Exit Slips Learning Log	
Week Two	Research	Graphic Organizer Learning Log Quiz: Pollination/ Bee Vocabulary	
Week Three	Application of Research Information Design Process	Planning Sheets Learning Log Quiz: Design Process	
Week Four	Product Creation	Rubric Quiz: Science Concepts Learning Log	
Week Five	Public Audience	Rubric Learning Log Test: Science Concepts	

You are exactly right if you are thinking, this is backward design. Correct! We have to know what standards we want to address in a PBL unit and at the same time figure out what it should look like when students learn those standards and ideas. The best way I can do that is to think ahead and map out my assessment plan before we start or at least in the first days of a new unit.

Assessment isn't a bad word! In fact, we are going to see assessment as our guide on this PBL journey. There is no need to stay up at night worrying if all this fun stuff we are doing in the classroom is going to pay off in the end! Being intentional about our assessment plan and weaving authentic tools into our PBL experience only makes the learning richer! Assessment provides accountability and helps us guide our students along the PBL journey. Audience is another critical piece of the PBL puzzle. The students do incredible work and thinking in a PBL unit, but without an authentic audience we lose motivation and momentum. Let's take a moment to consider the importance of an authentic audience.

Audience

I have never been an athlete, but I do love watching college football and the Olympics. I think about the endless hours of practice and conditioning the athletes endure in order to compete at such a high level. I think about the hard work, the sacrifices, and the importance of an audience to cheer them on. Yes, it is true that athletes compete against themselves and reach for their own goals, but they need a crowd to pump them up! Audience is key to sports, the arts, writing, or work. We all are just a little bit more motivated when we know someone else is going to see our final products or attend our performance.

Authentic audience is one of the pivotal elements of PBL. Without an authentic audience, students often wonder why they are doing the work or who really cares about the important information they have learned. Choosing the right audience is necessary in our PBL units. Just having lots of people see the students' work is not the goal. We want the right people to not only view the work, but be able to speak to the work and provide feedback.

I ask my students as we work through a unit to think about two things:

1. Who cares about the work we are doing in this unit?
2. Who can provide feedback for our work?

This pushes students beyond an open house mentality, and they begin to consider the school, community, national, or international audience that should be invited into our learning. Each PBL unit provides a unique audience. Consider some of the following audiences for past PBL units:

- Experts in a field (conservationist, architect, doctor, entrepreneur)
- School leadership

- Community leaders
- Nonprofit organization leaders or employees
- Students from different grade levels
- Students from another school in a different city, state, or country
- Contests or competitions
- University professors
- Social media influencers
- Professionals in the creative or fine arts
- Trade professionals
- Family and friends

Technology can be a great asset to providing authentic audience. Students can share their products, presentations, and solutions on a school website or social media platform. Photos or videos can be posted to engage the audience. Live presentations can be shared with audience members using videoconferencing. Following all school and district technology and privacy policies is necessary when posting student work and engaging with an audience, but it allows us to safely share the work and get useful feedback from experts.

Mandi Dimitriadis stresses the importance of authentic audience.

> PBL lends itself to authentic contexts for learning experiences, and authentic audiences for students to demonstrate their learning and receive feedback.
>
> If students are working with, or know they will be sharing their learning with, a real audience, they feel a sense of purpose. They know that someone else cares about what they are doing and feel motivated to create something they feel proud of.
>
> PBL is a powerful way for students to develop empathy for others by developing deep insights and understanding of how another person experiences the world. To be creating

a solution for someone else that you care about and have empathy for is incredibly motivating for students.

An authentic audience can provide students with genuine feedback that they can learn and grow from. In effect, the audience provides a teaching or mentoring role, building on what the classroom teacher is already doing.

By sharing learning with an authentic audience, students feel a sense of community and belonging that is a powerful motivator.

Knowing that they will be sharing their work with an authentic audience helps student feel a sense of commitment to the work, and they are more likely to set high standards for themselves.

Tracy Harris explains a recent project in which the audience was essential to the success of the project.

When we were building the farmers market stand outside, the school district's facilities department came to the school and started digging in the wrong area. We asked them to cover it back up, but they didn't fix it correctly. It caused a whole erosion issue that was going out onto the playground, which was perfectly tied to our science standards. We were teaching erosion at the time, so we had to come up with a way to fix that area to stop the soil from washing away. So the students started researching erosion and options of what could happen and what we would need to fix that whole entire area. The students came up with their own solutions of all different kinds. I let them come up with what they wanted to design. They had to come up with materials. They had to figure out how much it would cost, they had to put a presentation together. We had to present it to the leadership team, community members, and a landscaper that was going to help us cover the cost.

From that, the students decided they would also need landscaping, so in math class we talked about area, perimeter, and volume. The project expanded to include landscaping, so we had to figure out how much dirt we needed to bring in to the area. How much rock did we need? What type of plants would work best? We tied in as many standards as we could. The students used an online landscaping tool to develop their plans. The students designed the most cost-effective landscaping plans and then presented to all the sixth-grade classes. We selected the best design out of the presentations so all the sixth-grade students could work together on the landscaping.

I feel like when we do PBL this way, it is so much more impactful for my students.

An authentic audience can make or break our PBL units. If we want students to experience real learning and see how their work matters, we must invite experts, supporters, community members, and allies into our classrooms. Assessment provides accountability and an authentic audience motivates students to produce high-quality products and presentations. We need both to solidify the learning in our PBL units.

LIVE IT! LEARN IT! LOVE IT!

- Focus on individual growth and learning rather than group grades.

- Use a variety of assessment tools from beginning to end of a PBL unit to provide a true picture of each student's learning.

- Be OK with giving quizzes and tests to check for understanding. Don't overdo them, but use periodically to see where everyone is with the standards.

- Conferring and providing feedback are the best ways to monitor student progress. Make them a priority!

- Grades are not the goal, but part of the game we play. Accept the reality.

- Make an authentic audience a priority and involve students into the process of determining the audience.

- PBL Goes Virtual: Use helpful technology tools such as Kahoot!, Quizizz, or Quizlet for content and standard checkpoints. Have students share checklists, exit slips, and other documents using Seesaw, Google Classroom, Canvas, etc.

PBL PREP

f I had to choose between taking a vacation or buying décor for my house, I would take the trip every time! In fact, I've made that choice over and over in my life. Vacations with family and friends have always been a priority. One of my favorite parts of taking a vacation is prepping for the trip. The anticipation grows as I figure out the logistics, book the lodging, choose my outfits, pack the suitcases, and map out the adventure. I like to go with the flow, but basic preparation makes the trip more enjoyable. I have what I need to fully embrace the time away.

Just as we prepare for vacations, we should also prepare for PBL. I am not referring to planning the unit, but rather preparing our students for this unique type of learning experience. At this point in our discussion, you are probably feeling confident about implementing PBL at some level. I hope I have helped answer your burning questions and you feel ready to jump right into a unit with your class. As much as I love the enthusiasm, I am going to ask you to ponder something else before taking the leap.

Are your students prepared for PBL? I don't think there is a perfect time to do PBL, and I also don't think we should avoid PBL because of the excuse, "My students can't handle PBL." Somewhere in the middle, we recognize that we can in fact prepare students for this PBL journey.

WHY PBL PREP?

Even though we may not fully arrive at our first PBL unit with all these characteristics intact, we want to strive to provide a classroom environment that nurtures curiosity, student choice, and risk taking. I would also like for you to consider what can happen if we don't prepare students for the PBL experience.

Mr. I Will Teach My Way runs a very strict classroom. He has high expectations for his students and is an expert in his content. He tends to spend most of his instruction time lecturing. The students sit in rows and take notes as he delivers the content. He is entertaining and for the most part, students pay attention. He assigns homework and rarely has students interact with each other. He asks questions throughout his instruction but seeks only the right answers. He likes everything organized, neat, and tidy. His students do well on assessments, and he has decent state assessment scores. We like Mr. I Will Teach My Way.

Mr. I Will Teach My Way has been told he needs to include a PBL unit during the school year. He chooses to wait until spring when he feels he can loosen up on his curriculum. (I know we have chatted about PBL being the way we learn standards, but Mr. I Will Teach My Way hasn't quite internalized that yet. He still sees PBL as an "extra thing.") On a sunny Monday morning, he announces to his students that they will be doing a PBL unit and they will be working in groups. He decides to let them select their groups. This process is awkward and noisy. He begins to feel very uncomfortable. Mr. I Will Teach My Way presents the essential question for the unit, "How can we design a new football stadium to seat more people and adhere to a budget?" He asks the students for ideas and suggestions. He hears crickets. The students look at each other, trying to figure out what the teacher wants them to do. From this point, Mr. I Will Teach My Way goes down a very rocky path. He shakes his head every day, muttering, "I told you this wasn't going to work."

PBL prep matters. The students in Mr. I Will Teach My Way had little to no experience with the skill set needed for PBL. They were being asked to immediately switch from total teacher-directed instruction to student-centered learning, and it was too much of a chasm to span. We must set the stage for PBL by sprinkling PBL prep elements throughout our instruction and across the weeks. We want Mr. I Will Teach My Way to succeed with PBL, and we want to have our own success. PBL prep leads to this goal.

Teachers and students from the alternative high school and main high school campus collaborated to sponsor an art auction of student-made birdhouses. The students in the construction-skills course at the alternative high school designed and built the birdhouses. They passed them on to the art class students to paint using famous paintings as their inspiration. The birdhouses were auctioned off as a fund raiser for the district's education foundation.

So Lori, are you saying that I have to do these types of things all the time? Yes! Isn't it awesome? PBL not only changes learning for students, but it seems to have this magical way of changing us as teachers. We begin to integrate more of the PBL elements into our daily routines because it just makes sense. We give more choice, have more dialogue, present more challenges, and allow students to own their learning.

Please do not misunderstand—I am not saying wait until every member of your class is highly functioning with each of the PBL prep elements. Instead, let's be intentional about embedding PBL elements into our instruction from day one of school so that we can begin our PBL unit by the end of the first quarter, if not earlier.

Another reason for doing our best to integrate PBL prep into our first weeks of school is because we recognize that students can only juggle so many skills and tasks at once. If we ask students to not only wrestle with the PBL challenge, while also learning to work with others, do research, manage time, create a product, and share with an audience, we are going to see students struggle. It is too much! Multitasking is pretty much a myth. Our brains can only really focus on one new thing at a time. However, if we prime the pump with all the social skills and PBL prep elements, students only have to stay focused on the content of the PBL unit.

PBL PREP QUIZ

Consider the following questions. Think about where you are in your school year and which of these experiences your students have engaged in so far.

1. How would you describe your classroom community? Do students know the names of their peers? Does everyone treat each other with respect for the most part?

2. Have you used cooperative learning in your instruction? Are students used to working with someone else?

3. How have you used inquiry to stretch your students' thinking? Do you use STEM/STEAM activities or design process? Have students had an opportunity to try, fail, try again, and take academic risks?

4. Have you sprinkled small research tasks throughout your curriculum so students are comfortable asking questions and looking for answers?

5. Are students comfortable and proficient using the technology tools you have available?

6. Do the students understand your expectations for behavior in the classroom and can they appropriately use supplies and time? Are students comfortable with moving around the room and rotating to stations or centers?

7. How much student choice have you extended in your instruction? Are students used to making choices, sharing their thoughts, and making suggestions?

Now that you have considered your own instructional practices, let's see how this relates to PBL prep. Each of the questions above illustrate the types of experiences necessary to build the foundation for PBL in the classroom.

PBL prep is my term for providing the experiences you just pondered prior to the first PBL unit. There is no perfect classroom, and students continue to grow and mature with each new learning challenge. We may not be able to address all the prep pieces, but intentionally building into our first weeks of school these strategies paves the way to a successful first PBL unit.

We need to intentionally integrate the following strategies and experiences into our first weeks of school in order to prepare for project-based learning.

PBL PREP CHECKLIST

	Classroom Community
	Cooperative Learning/Collaboration
	Inquiry/STEM/STEAM/Critical Thinking
	Small Research Tasks/Asking Questions/ Finding Answers
	Technology Tools
	Understanding Expectations: Movement, Supplies, Time
	Student Choice

Essential Question: What can we invent to make a daily task easier?

Content Areas: Science and Communication Arts

Students became inventors and designed inventions that would make a daily task easier for students their own age. Students surveyed others about their daily tasks and needs. They researched products already available and brainstormed their own inventions.

> Students learned the design process while working through the unit. They shared their invention prototypes and presentation with business owners during a *Shark Tank*-style culminating event.

PBL AND THE CLASSROOM DYNAMIC

PBL work involves communication, risk-taking, collaboration, and critical thinking. A positive and supportive classroom community is absolutely necessary for PBL success. Relationships are always crucial, and we must be very intentional about building relationships with the individual students in our classes and providing opportunities for students to bond with one another. A classroom community is not built immediately with a day or two of back-to-school icebreakers. We need to do icebreakers and getting-to-know-you activities, but we will not create the safe environment we desire overnight. Community is built over time and with intention. Here are a few of my favorite ways to connect with students and develop the type of learning environment that serves PBL well.

Greeting Students

Many of us remember purchasing the book, *The First Days of School*, by Harry Wong. This essential guidebook to all things teaching has helped millions of teachers wrap our head around classroom management. One of the tidbits in the book that really resonated with me from the get-go was the notion of greeting students at the door every day, every class period. Rather than fiddling around getting ready for class at my desk, I would wait by the door to greet my often-rambunctious students with a smile and a genuine welcome. I complimented new haircuts, called folks by name, and looked for those who needed a little extra hug to start the day.

This practice is not rocket science; it is just good teaching. I have seen many examples on social media of teachers jazzing this ritual up with special handshakes, nicknames, dances, even confetti. That's awesome, but don't get lost in the novelty. The reason for making this one-to-one connection is clear: we want to build positive relationships with students. We want them to know that we care and are truly excited they are in our class. We want them to feel safe and valued.

We keep this in mind when teaching virtually. We greet our students through Zoom or in a video each day so we can "see" each other. We learn names and faces. We play fun games together synchronously to get to know our likes, dislikes, and interests. We focus on the social-emotional learning part of virtual instruction and make it a daily priority.

Morning Meeting/Responsive Advisory Meeting

One of the best professional development trainings I have ever attended is the Responsive Classroom institute (responsiveclassroom.org). It is absolutely energizing, affirming, and practical. Responsive Classroom is an evidence-based approach to teaching and discipline that focuses on engaging academics, positive community, effective management, and developmental awareness. One of the key components in the Responsive Classroom approach is the implementation of Morning Meeting or Responsive Advisory Meeting, depending on the grade level, each day. These informal class meetings set the stage for learning. These can be done face-to-face or virtually. Students are made to feel welcome and activities are used to engage students and build community. The meetings are structured and efficient, but oh-so powerful!

Morning Meeting Structure (Elementary)

- Greeting
- Sharing
- Group activity
- Morning message

Responsive Advisory Meeting (Secondary)

- Arrival welcome
- Announcements
- Acknowledgments
- Activity

In a few moments at the beginning of a class or class period, we can connect with students, meet socio-emotional needs, get learners thinking, laughing, and smoothly transitioning into instruction. I have learned through doing Morning Meetings that "The class that plays together, stays together." If you are worried about having time to do meetings, let me assure you that the few minutes you invest in a meeting will save you hundreds of minutes redirecting behavior throughout the year. It really is that impactful! I urge you to check out Responsive Classroom and learn more about Morning and Responsive Advisory Meetings!

OUTSIDE THE SCHOOL WALLS

I am going to suggest something next that might seem a bit farfetched for some, and I totally understand. It may seem unnecessary and certainly inconvenient. Bear with me. I have found that relationships and class community is often built outside the school walls. Many of my connections with students were sealed by attending a Mighty Mites football game, ballet recital, or school carnival. Obviously we can't attend every activity our students are involved in, but if we are savvy . . . we can attend a few that really matter.

At the beginning of the school year, I surveyed my students to find out what types of activities and sports my students enjoyed. Some didn't take dance lessons or play sports, so I learned about their hobbies and interests instead. I would then strategically plan to attend a few key events early in the school year that involved multiple students. I was lucky. In my community the parks department schedules multiple football, soccer, volleyball, and basketball games on the same day. I would carve out a night to watch soccer and see many of my students participating in the games. I might take a Saturday morning and head to the community gym to watch a few rounds of volleyball and wave at my girls. It is amazing how far some eye contact, a wave, and a "Go, Eagles" yell will go to building a strong bond in the classroom. I also headed to the school carnivals, book fairs, Boy Scout Pinewood Derbies, and high school football games as often as I could because invariably, I would see my students. It let my students see me as a person, not just a teacher. It told them, without saying a word, that I valued them and their interests. The little bit of time I sacrificed paid off immensely in the classroom. I have found it true that "People don't care how much you know, until they know how much you care."

> One of the best things I remember about your class was how I knew how much you cared about me. You were always looking for ways to help me be successful. Whether that came from a new learning opportunity or just taking time to show me how much you cared.
>
> –Morgan Kelly

I want to be realistic. I have a family and my own life. I love teaching and my students, but balance is everything. I am not suggesting we fill our calendars, running to every ballgame, play, or robotics tournament involving our students. I am also not encouraging us to put ourselves in awkward situations. However, there is an appropriate middle ground that allows us to build positive relationships with students that will blossom in the classroom.

CONCLUSION

So, what will your PBL prep timeline look like? How will you purposely incorporate the PBL prep elements in your classroom prior to your first PBL unit? How will you nurture these elements throughout the school year? I hope you are beginning to see the big picture. PBL is not a one-and-done. It is a mindset! And that mindset doesn't just reside in your students, but in you as well. Here's how my colleague Tracy Harris put it:

> I have always been a person that does not like to do the same thing all the time. Even with the twenty-three years

I have been teaching, I can honestly say that maybe there has been a project that I have done twice, but I have done it a different way. I don't like to be stagnant with what I do because that would be boring for myself, and then I am not pushing myself to be better for my kids. Everybody is different and every class is different. We are always trying to improve. We are still trying to figure out how we can be innovative and what we can be doing to push our kids, but also continue to push ourselves.

PBL doesn't just impact your entire instructional plan because we are prepping for it and spreading the elements of PBL throughout our days and year—it literally changes the way we teach. It is no longer a stand-alone but becomes "the way we do business."

LIVE IT! LEARN IT! LOVE IT!

- PBL prep is the intentional integration of key skills and strategies into our instruction in preparation for our first PBL unit.

	Classroom Community
	Cooperative Learning/Collaboration
	Inquiry/STEM/STEAM/Critical Thinking
	Small Research Tasks/Asking Questions/Finding Answers
	Technology Tools
	Understanding Expectations: Movement, Supplies, Time
	Student Choice

- PBL Goes Virtual: We provide the same types of experiences virtually for PBL prep. We especially focus on community building and familiarity with essential tech tools early in the school year. We provide lots of opportunities for students to make choices.

MAKING TIME FOR PBL

Hopefully you are now convinced this PBL idea is worth pursuing. One of the next questions that is most likely circling around your racing thoughts is WHEN? When in the world will you fit this exciting possibility into your already overcrowded day? I hear you!

Time seems to be one of the biggest issues with starting PBL, and honestly, everything in education. "When do you do project-based learning?" and "How do you fit it in?" These are important questions that weigh heavily on the minds of educators wanting to go in this direction. Let's first remind ourselves that PBL is not in addition to what we are already expected to teach. We address and teach a selected group of standards through our PBL units. Once we recognize this, it is much easier to figure out the time issue. If we view PBL as HOW we will teach our existing standards, instead of just one more thing to do, we have a much easier time seeing where it fits.

I would like to help with the time concern by asking you to reflect on your current schedule and practice.

- How much time do you usually spend on a unit, chapter, concept?

- What type of activities and lessons are involved in the process? (Lecture, independent practice, assessments, projects, etc.)
- How much of your instructional period or day is consumed by the unit, chapter, or concept?
- How successful are the students with the key concepts with this approach?
- Is there any additional time during your day or week that you use in a flexible way? (Perhaps you provide a study hall on Fridays, or choice time each afternoon in an elementary classroom.)

TEACH THIS, NOT THAT!

Now we will use your reflection to carve out a plan for PBL. What I hear you saying is that you do map out time for teaching concepts and required standards, so instead of struggling with adding PBL to your schedule, think about doing an instructional swap. You will still teach the same things but choose PBL instead of your regular instructional plans for the same concepts.

Maybe this will help clarify. I really like David Zinczenko's *Eat This, Not That!* books. Have you seen them? They are colorful and have awesome pictures and graphics of something I love . . . food! The premise of his books is to show the reader the healthiest options for any given meal. Let's say I am craving Mexican food. I have a hankering for chips, guac, and something really spicy. You aren't going to change my mind. I don't want kale. I don't want grilled salmon. I have earned the right to some comfort food this week, and you better believe I am diving in! I open one of Zinczenko's books and he shows me in gorgeous photos what would be the healthiest option at my favorite Mexican restaurant. Eat this, not that! I still have Mexican food, but I make a wise choice.

This is exactly what we are doing with PBL. It is Teach This, Not That. We are choosing to devote the time we were already using in this way instead of how we did it before. We won't always choose PBL as the method of instruction, but when we do, we simply choose this, not that.

Essential Question: How can we teach elementary students about earth science?

Content Area: Science

High school students were challenged with teaching fifth-grade students basic earth science concepts. They were challenged to take what they were learning and find a way to make it interesting and applicable to younger students. To further the challenge, the high school students would be using Skype for the teaching sessions. They had to develop activities and presentations that would engage learners through live streaming. The fifth-grade students served as the authentic audience and provided feedback on the content and method of instruction.

How can we justify this swap? Remember that we are not teaching standards or concepts first and then adding an additional PBL unit to address those same standards or concepts. Rather, we are choosing to teach and learn the group of standards while implementing the PBL unit. We allot time just as we would for any other unit, chapter, or study, but the PBL unit replaces the original means of teaching the same set of standards.

Middle and High School

For middle school and high school teachers, I think the instructional swap idea is easy to grasp. Choose this, not that just means blocking off a certain number of class periods to engage in the PBL unit. Sometimes it isn't a seamless swap, but manageable. If you have a block schedule, you may want to use part of the block for other curriculum goals and the second half of the block for PBL work. You may want to devote the full block for a couple of weeks to your PBL unit. It is up to you, and it will work! Your units may get tricky if you are collaborating with other teachers. Maybe you teach science and your colleague teaches writing. You will need to meet often to discuss how the unit will be split between your two classes. It might mean that early in the unit your science students do the experiments and research and then the writing teacher facilitates the writing and presentation pieces in his class. Teamwork makes the dream work!

Middle School/High School (50-Minute Classes)

- Use the full fifty minutes for the PBL unit because this is how you are teaching those standards. Create a timeline so no time is wasted.

Middle School/High School (Block Scheduling)

- Use part of the block for the PBL unit and the other part of the block for additional lessons.

Elementary Research Workshop

Elementary teachers have different time constraints and lots of curricula to juggle. Time is the enemy, and even when we choose the this, not that strategy, we have loose ends we need to tie up. One way I like to address this is to introduce the concept of a research workshop.

When I first started teaching, I was, for the most part, in control of my schedule. I was told when lunch, recess, and special classes would occur, but everything else was up to me. That freedom came to a screeching halt a few years later, when mandates, state assessments, and new programs were added to my plate. I woke up to a new world where I was expected to follow a scope-and-sequence chart, new math series, and include a block of time for literacy each morning. My schedule was no longer my own, and I had to make some choices.

> It is crazy to me that I remember all the projects we created because I don't have vivid memories from my other grade school years.
>
> —Lauren Miller Petit

I knew that our learning with PBL and other inquiry-based approaches were working, so I searched for a way to have my cake and eat it too! I noticed that there was a chunk of time each afternoon that I could spend 30–45 minutes on social studies, science, and anything else that needed to be covered. I started calling this afternoon time research workshop. It provided me with a lovely chunk of the day I could use to integrate social studies, science, and the other content areas if necessary in authentic learning such as PBL. This helped me make better connections for students and gave me more time to do what needed to be done.

My research workshop is based on the basic workshop model:

- Mini-Lesson/Modeling/Setting Expectations (5–10 minutes)
- Students Work/Teacher Confers with Students (25–35 minutes)
- Reflection/Goal Setting for the Next Day of Work (3–5 minutes)

Not only does research workshop provide extra time for PBL units, it organizes our time in a scaffolded and structured way. No chaos happening here, just using the most of every minute!

In addition to research workshop, I used my instructional-swap idea, using that block of time to incorporate PBL in whatever content area was being addressed in my PBL unit. To better visualize this, peek into this elementary classroom with me!

Self-Contained Elementary Classroom

Ms. I Heart Second Grade is a huge fan of PBL. Her adorable second graders are with her all day, except for special classes such as art, music, PE. She has some flexibility with her schedule. However, her school requires a 90-minute literacy block and 60 minutes of math instruction daily. She also has students that receive special services throughout the day. Even with these timing issues, she rocks PBL.

She took my advice and uses her afternoon block for social studies/science as a research workshop. This gives her 30–45 minutes daily she can use for either PBL or another awesome type of learning such as STEM, inquiry, research, hands-on experiences, etc. Most of her PBL units address either social studies or science standards so this block of time daily works well when she is engaging in a unit.

Even with this chunk of time each afternoon, it is not quite possible to get everything accomplished in her unit, she will need to use some time earlier in the day to integrate all of her content standards. For example, her class is learning about plants and soil in her latest PBL unit. She is focusing on science standards, but she is also incorporating nonfiction reading and writing.

This is her schedule during the unit:

8:15–8:30	Morning Routine/Morning Meeting
8:30–9:30	Guided Reading Block (Some PBL focus) Students continue in small guided reading groups and station rotations. She incorporates some nonfiction texts about plants and soil when appropriate and reads high-interest books about plants/soil during her shared reading on some days. Students continue their normal routine of working on vocabulary, reading software programs, and reading with a partner during the rotations.
9:30–9:45	Recess
9:45–10:30	Math (No PBL focus)
10:30–11:00	Music
11:00–11:40	Writer's Workshop (Some PBL focus) She focuses on nonfiction writing during workshop so students can use those skills to write their own nonfiction pieces for the PBL unit.
11:40–12:05	Lunch
12:05–12:20	Recess
12:20–12:40	Independent Reading/Conferring (No PBL focus)
12:40–1:25	Word Work and Literacy Rotations (No PBL focus)
1:25–1:40	Recess
1:40–2:15	Math Rotations/End of Day Routine (No PBL focus)
2:15–3:00	Research Workshop: Social Studies & Science (PBL Unit) Students are engaged in research, experiments, and creating their presentations and products during this time.

Ms. I Heart Second Grade does a beautiful job weaving PBL into her day and still continues with her routines and other content. Sounds good, but what if you teach in a departmentalized setting? No worries. We can check out another classroom for inspiration.

Departmentalized Elementary Classroom

Mr. Fifth Grade Is Where I Wanna Be teaches math and science and his teaching partner focuses on reading, writing, and social studies. The first half of the day he teaches his homeroom students then they switch classes. The day is divided into two large blocks of time. This works pretty well for most things, but PBL is a bit more challenging. He and his teaching partner plan together so that they make sure all the curriculum is not only being taught, but is engaging and authentic to the fifth graders.

Most of their PBL units involve two content areas. Currently, the fifth graders are learning about government. They have interviewed local government officials and decided to find a solution to a growing problem with traffic in the city. They are researching, devising solutions, and will make proposals for fixing this frustrating problem to city leaders in a few weeks. The students will be learning social studies concepts and design process standards for science. Students will do part of the project in Mr. Fifth Grade Is Where I Wanna Be's classroom and the other sections in the co-teacher's class.

To manage the time, the teachers agree on the following time schedule:

Weeks 1–2 of the PBL Unit: Use social studies time to learn city policies and more about the traffic issues. Students will research solutions and needed information.

Weeks 3–4: Use the science block to design solutions for the traffic issue based on the research done in the previous weeks. Students will prepare presentations to share with city leaders.

Week 5: Students will share their plans and presentations with the social studies/communication arts teacher for critique, reflection, and revision.

Week 6: Present findings to city leaders

Both teachers are involved, but neither is spending the entire day on the PBL unit. The division of work and learning is based on the content areas and standards selected.

Fourth-grade students honored firefighters who fought the brush fires in the area surrounding their school. Students created various products and presentations to thank the emergency responders for their help and bravery. The students invited the firefighters to the school for a special ceremony and reception.

DEADLINES AND CALENDARS

Time management is key in PBL. If we don't time the unit just right, we might drag the project out until everyone is over it. Or we cram too much learning into an unrealistically short time frame, forcing us into panic mode. Let's try to avoid both. First, I say, "Go old school!" Get out your desk calendar. Take into consideration the steps in the PBL implementation process we discussed. Also, consider the time you have available for PBL each day. Map out on the calendar how many days you estimate each step taking based on the time constraints under which you are operating. A reality check takes place when see our instructional days laid out in front of us.

Next, set a few deadlines. Decide when you want the public audience day to be. Give yourself enough time to get there, but not so much time so that students lose interest and momentum. Look again at your calendar and think about when the research piece should be completed and when you want to do the first round of prep and rehearsal. Pencil those deadlines in also. Make the calendar visible to students once you have started the unit. Some teachers find creating a PBL wall helpful. You can post your essential question, charts, and calendars, etc., in one location. Setting deadlines and posting a calendar creates an authentic urgency to get things done!

LIVE IT! LEARN IT! LOVE IT!

- Time is one of our biggest concerns; there never seems to be enough of it. However, we can use our time for PBL when we really understand its purpose, benefits, and realities within our own classroom schedules.

- Use the Teach This, Not That swapping strategy for addressing your standards in the unit.

- Consider designating time for a research workshop in your schedule.

- Collaborate with other teachers to divide and conquer!

- Integrate mini-lessons and modeling into the content areas being addressed for each unit.

- Map out the unit on a calendar and set deadlines.

- PBL Goes Virtual: Use the same Teach This, Not That strategy to help you organize your unit timeline.

PBL GOES VIRTUAL

Writing this book has been such a dream come true for me! I have been anxiously awaiting the opportunity to share my PBL journey through a resource for teachers for a long time. I had no way of knowing how crazy the path would be from my dream to this reality.

Just as I was finishing the manuscript for *Project-Based Learning Anywhere*, the world literally changed overnight. I took a ten-day trip to the beautiful Gulf Coast to write the final chapters of the book and returned home to face a new world because of COVID-19. Travel came to a complete stop and my support to teachers and administrators shifted from normal professional development to unprecedented problem-solving online.

As educators, we were faced with the unimaginable tasks of teaching our students virtually and comforting families while we ourselves were overwhelmed with the unbelievable circumstances taking place. I will admit openly that I do not have all the answers about how to translate project-based learning into a virtual environment, but I have some hunches based on the successes through the pandemic. I have tried to address the ever-present elephant in the room regarding how we take PBL virtual throughout this book. For good or bad, I do believe we will be relying on virtual/hybrid/blended learning for a long time, even when things return to normal. Whatever "normal" is?

I did worry early on during this unprecedented time about whether PBL would withstand this shift to a virtual environment. I was concerned that teachers would be too overwhelmed to consider PBL as a way to reach students and make the content come alive for them. However, I am actually seeing a surge of interest! We have learned that teaching virtually is a whole different ball game, and engaging students is literally exhausting using synchronous/asynchronous instruction. We are desperately seeking ways to engage, inspire, and empower learners. Thankfully, PBL is here to help us!

More good news for PBL lovers is that we can take our step-by-step approach to PBL and use some of the technology tools we have become familiar with recently and easily adapt them for our purposes. Just so we are all on the same page, let me quickly define two phrases I will use in the step-by-step approach:

- *Videoconferencing*: Using a technology tool such as Zoom, Google Meet, Teams, or Skype to communicate with students in real time.
- *Online Class Home Base*: Using an online platform to post content for students and parents. This can be a learning-management system such as Canvas, Google Classroom, or Schoology. It might be a class website or Seesaw. This is the location for your lessons, videos, assignments, etc.

Let's see how PBL might look like virtually.

Teacher Prep #1: Identify the Standards

We are at our best when using standards as our starting point. There's no reason why that shouldn't be the case virtually.

Teacher Prep #2: Formulate the Challenge

Write your essential question and formulate the challenge.

Step One: Project Launch

Launch the project using tech tools to hook the students and build background knowledge. You might post a video for students to view and discuss. You could provide a virtual field trip so students learn more about a location or situation. Guest speakers and experts could Zoom/Google Meet/Skype/Teams, etc., with students to get them interested in the challenge or topic.

Step Two: Challenge and Essential Question

Share the challenge and essential question with students through video-conferencing and a discussion with the class. You will want to post the challenge and essential question to your class online home base.

Step Three: Chart Questions/Need-to-Knows/ Need-to-Dos

Meet with students in small groups to develop the chart of questions/ need-to-knows/need-to-dos. These small-group conversations can be done using discussion boards like Padlet or using a Google document. You can meet virtually using videoconferencing. Then share the final chart with everyone via your online home base.

Step Four: Mini-Lessons, Modeling, and Scaffolding

Build the foundation for the unit by sharing mini-lessons and modeling. You can use tools such as Nearpod, Seesaw, and Google Classroom to post videos, lessons, and tutorials. Share your mini-lessons using the technology tool you are using for all your online instruction.

Step Five: Research and Conferring

Students can begin researching using high-quality online resources you select and share. You can provide links on your class online home base site, create a digital choice board, or share many links at once by using a bookmarking site such as Symbaloo.

Step Six: Work Days and Conferring

Once students have completed their research, they will most likely need to create digital products. Here are some of my favorite creativity tools:

- Adobe Spark: Video, Web Page, and Post Creator
- Seesaw: Video, Audio Recording, Drawing, Writing, Typing Tool
- Book Creator: Digital-Book Creator
- Animoto: Slideshow and Video Creator
- Google Slides/Google Docs: Presentation and Writing Tools
- Canva: Graphic Design Tool

Conferences can be held with individuals or groups using video-conferencing tools.

Step Seven: Prep and Rehearsal

Students can present their products to the teacher and other students to receive feedback prior to sharing with the public audience. Video tools such as Flipgrid, Seesaw, and Zoom are perfect for sharing and receiving feedback.

Step Eight: Public Audience/Sharing

This step can be a little tricky because of privacy issues. You may not want to have your students show their homes in real time with your audience. It is probably best to use video with a neutral background or audio-only recordings of presentations to share with your audience. You can share the videos/audio recordings/products directly with your audience or on your class online home base site for others to see/hear. Feedback from the audience is important. They can respond through email, video using something like Flipgrid, discussion boards, etc.

Step Nine: Reflection

Students can reflect on the project and the feedback in writing, conversation, or in a survey. They can type a reflection using Microsoft Word or Google Docs, record their thoughts in Seesaw or Flipgrid, or complete a survey using Google Forms or SurveyMonkey.

Essential Question: Do we still value the American dream?

Content Area: English

HIGH SCHOOL
– PBL UNIT –

High school students were challenged to discover if people today recognize, value, and pursue the American dream. Students interacted with various community leaders who valued the American dream and some who felt the American dream was no longer an obtainable goal. The students did their own research, surveys, and interviews with chosen groups. They compiled their findings in a written piece and shared the results with the experts who had visited earlier in the unit. They also posted their results on the school social media accounts for the community to read.

I know you are probably thinking, "This looks good, but there are lots of 'what ifs?' in this solution." You are exactly right! What if students don't have devices or equal access to technology? What if students don't buy in to the project? What if I can't use Zoom or other synchronous types of technology tools? The list goes on and on. I get it! Moving our instruction online really takes a lot of control out of our hands and it drives us crazy. Rightly so.

If students do not have access to technology, we can provide research articles and materials on paper for students to use during the projects. Instead of digital products, we have students create models or artwork from materials found at home. If you are unable to use videoconferencing or other types of synchronous (in real time) tools, post recorded videos, images, and documents on your class online home base for students to view and use when needed.

If you are concerned about students collaborating or not buying in to the project, consider having individual students choose their own "passion project" to explore and share based on their passion, interest, or expertise. Students develop questions based on their passion, research, and create a product to share a presentation with others that demonstrates their understanding of the passion topic. This can easily be done by individual students or by small groups of students working virtually.

When considering PBL units for virtual learning, brainstorm current events, problems in the community, or opportunities to educate others about a relevant topic. Some examples of virtual PBL projects:

- Design challenges (design a new mask, needed invention, or new building design)
- Projects based on surveying or polling (a business is most needed in the community)
- Projects that educate about a cause or needed information (creating PSAs, video tutorials, or ebooks about healthy eating)
- Debates (showing both sides of an issue, such as the appropriate age to drive or vote)
- Experiments (growing plants in various at home environments)
- Simulations (students take on a role such as travel guide or travel writer and document their journey)

The best we can do is to utilize the resources we have in the most effective ways possible. We know project-based learning empowers our students. We also know that teachers and students are creative and innovative. As we keep our eyes on the prize of authentic learning, the roadblocks may seem a little bit smaller as we continue our PBL journey online.

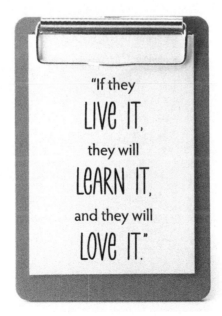

"If they **LIVE IT**, they will **LEARN IT**, and they will **LOVE IT**."

APPENDICES

Appendix A: *Brainstorming and Planning Sheets*

DREAM BIG!	
Standards I Need to Teach	What Does This Look Like in the Real World?
What If? Project Ideas	Resources I Already Have

PBL PLANNING: STEP BY STEP

Step One: Project Launch

Step Two: Challenge & Essential Question

Step Three: Questions/Need to Know/Need to Do Chart

Step Four: Mini-Lesson/Modeling

Step Five: Research

Step Six: Students Work & Teacher Confers with Students

Step Seven: Prep & Rehearsal

Step Eight: Big Event/Sharing with a Real Audience

Step Nine: Reflection

Appendix B: PBL Prep Checklist

PBL PReP: TOOLS IN MY TOOLBOX	
TOOLS	IN MY TOOLBOX: THOUGHTS & NOTES
Build a Community	
Cooperative Learning	
Inquiry/STEM/STEAM	
Small Research Tasks: Gathering Information	
Technology/Activities	
Stations/Centers	
Student Choice	

Appendix C: Assessment Tools & Assessment Plan

FORMS OF ASSESSMENT: PROJECT-BASED LEARNING		
APPROPRIATE FOR THE UNIT	ASSESSMENT TOOLS	STANDARDS/PURPOSE
	Teacher Observations	
	Conference Notes	
	Learning Log/Project Journals or Notebooks	
	Exit Slips/ Formative Assessments	
	Checklists	
	Rubrics/Scoring Guides	
	Quizzes/Checkpoints	
	Unit Test	
	Written Reflections/ Products	
	Reflections Based on Photos at the End of the Unit	
	Student Plans and Task Management Sheets	

ASSESSMENT PLAN

PBL Unit:

TIMELINE	GOALS/STANDARDS	ASSESSMENTS	REFLECTIONS/NOTES

Appendix D: Selection of Standards

SELECTING STANDARDS
What standards are nonnegotiable? Students must master the skills/concepts in this grade level? The BIG ROCKS!
Which standards authentically connect with another content area's standards?
Look for clusters of standards in each subject area that naturally make sense together.
QUESTION TO ASK YOURSELF: ARE THESE STANDARDS WORTHY OF THE TIME INVOLVED IN THIS PROJECT?

Appendix E: PBL Checklist

SELF-REFLECTION: PBL UNIT PLANNING		
✓	MUST-HAVES	THOUGHTS/QUESTIONS
	My project is based on important standards or cluster of standards	
	I have written an Essential Question that is student friendly.	
	My project is real-world and students will have an authentic role or challenge	
	I know what to assess, when to assess, and how. I have my assessment timeline created.	
	Students will have choice and voice. I have included students in decision making throughout the project.	
	Students will learn as we work on the project, not just submit something at the end of the unit.	
	I will kick off the unit with a hook that gets everyone pumped about learning.	
	Students will be doing the work! They will be researching, planning, and creating.	
	I have built in mini-lessons and modeling to scaffold the learning.	
	I have planned for ongoing conferencing and will check in with students daily.	
	We have a public audience who appreciates the work.	
	I have created a project timeline and set deadlines.	

Appendix F: Conference Sheet

						Student Name	Understands the Essential Question	Topic Selection	Research	Planning of Product/ Presentation	Creation of Product/ Presentation	Prep & Rehearsal	Public Audience	Reflection

REFERENCES

Print

Bender, William. *Project-Based Learning: Differentiating Instruction for the 21st Century.* Thousand Oaks, CA: Corwin Press, 2012.

Boss, Suzanne K., and Jane A. Krauss. *Thinking Through Project-Based Learning: Guiding Deeper Inquiry.* Thousand Oaks, CA: Corwin Press, 2013.

Boss, Suzie, John Larmer, and John R. Mergendoller. *Setting the Standard for PBL.* Alexandria, VA: ASCD, 2015.

Duke, Nell K., Anne-Lise Halvorsen, Stephanie L. Strachan, Jihyun Kim, and Spyros Konstantopoulos. "Putting PBL to the Test: The Impact of Project-Based Learning on Second Graders' Social Studies and Literacy Learning and Motivation in Low-SES School Settings." *American Educational Research Journal* (June 8, 2020). https://doi.org/10.3102/0002831220929638.

Evans, C. M. *Student Outcomes from High-Quality Project-Based Learning: A Case Study for PBLWorks.* Dover, NH: Center for Assessment, 2019.

Kingston, S. *PBL & Student Achievement: What Does the Research Tell Us? PBL Evidence Matters.* 1, no. 1 (2018) 1–11.

McTighe, Jay, and Grant Wiggins. *Essential Questions: Opening Doors to Student Understanding.* Alexandria, VA: ASCD, 2013.

Wolpert-Gawron, Heather. *DIY Project Based Learning for ELA and History (Eye on Education).* New York: Routledge Publishing, 2015.

Wormeli, Rick. *Fair Isn't Always Equal: Assessment and Grading in the Differentiated Classroom.* Portland, ME: Stenhouse Publishers, 2018.

Websites

Bernard Marr: "The 10+ Most Important Job Skills Every
Company Will Be Looking For in 2020"

https://www.forbes.com/sites/bernardmarr/2019/10/28/the-10-most
-important-job-skills-every-company-will-be-looking-for-in
-2020/#6a6a95df67b6

John Spencer: http://www.spencerauthor.com

PBLWorks: https://www.pblworks.org/what-is-pbl

Responsive Classroom: https://www.responsiveclassroom.org

Sylvia Duckworth: https://www.edtechteam.com/blog/2018/08/
eduslam-how-to-sketchnote/

ACKNOWLEDGMENTS

Writing *Project-Based Learning Anywhere* has been an amazing experience! I so appreciate the Dave Burgess Consulting, Inc. team for the opportunity to share my PBL journey with the world. Thank you Dave, Shelley, Tara, Marisol, and Lindsey for all your support and encouragement. Because of your guidance, we were able to create the guidebook I desired teachers to have. I am incredibly honored and humbled to be a Pirate! Thank you for everything!

I am blessed to be part of such an encouraging, creative, loving, and hilarious family. My people give me the courage and drive to continue to live and learn! Much love and thanks to Tim, Austin, Ashlyn, and Ana for your support and inspiration every single day.

A big thanks to my colleagues, who happen to also be amazing friends! Your energy, wisdom, kindness, and professionalism make me a better person and educator. Thank you, Adam Peterson, Matt Halpern, Cheryl Dick, Deedee Wills, Shannon Cunningham, Sam Williams, Hilary Statum, Melissa Dickson, Kim Adsit, Laureen Reynolds, Emily Hawkins, my SDE and ESGI pals, and so many more for all the memories and opportunities to live and learn with you!

Thank you Mandi Dimitriadis and Tracy Harris for sharing your inspiring PBL stories and tips with us! I am beyond grateful for your willingness to be part of this project. I treasure your friendship and your insights!

I want to thank the educators across the country who have invited me to partner with them to plan and implement PBL in their classrooms. You are so talented, passionate, and enthusiastic about making learning real for your students. I can't thank you enough for all that you do to make school a great place to be!

Finally, big shoutouts to these outstanding educators who provided insight and feedback for *Project-Based Learning Anywhere*. I am so honored that you would help me with this project. I am in awe of your leadership, vision, and enthusiasm. Each of you brings so much joy and inspiration to my life!:

- Macaire McDonough-Davies, principal: Deerwood Elementary, Kingwood, Texas
- Scott Duncan, principal: Willow Creek, Kingwood, Texas
- Dr. Sarah Williams, director of instruction and accountability: Hampton County School District 2, Estill, South Carolina
- Carrie Harvey-Zales, assistant superintendent for Curriculum and Instruction, Plattsburgh City School District, Plattsburgh, New York
- Susana Lapeyrade-Drummond, associate superintendent of Curriculum and Instruction, Archdiocese of San Francisco Department of Catholic Schools

"If they live it, they will learn it, and they will love it!"

ABOUT THE AUTHOR

Dr. Lori Elliott is an enthusiastic and outstanding educator. She has served as a classroom teacher, technology integration specialist, and literacy coordinator during her almost thirty years in education. She currently serves as an educational consultant, content developer, and presenter.

Dr. Elliott is a former National Board-Certified teacher. She has a master's degree in reading and a doctorate in instructional leadership. She is a former eMINTS teacher/trainer and STARR teacher for the state of Missouri.

Dr. Lori is passionate about project-based learning, literacy, technology integration, and authentic learning. She has authored several books related to these topics. Lori believes building positive relationships with students, parents, and colleagues is the most important thing we can do as educators. Her energy and love for teaching and learning is contagious. Lori is well-known for providing humorous, engaging, and practical presentations. She partners with educators across the country and internationally to teach, learn, plan, and implement best instructional practices.

BRING DR. LORI TO YOUR SCHOOL!

Dr. Lori is an energetic presenter and skilled practitioner. Lori uses her years of experience and expertise to customize professional-development programs for schools and school districts. Her trainings are humorous, engaging, and highly practical. She understands the importance of ongoing professional learning and provides follow-up sessions for planning, collaborating, and coaching for both teachers and administrators. Lori believes relationships are key and loves to work alongside educators as they begin, continue, and celebrate their PBL journeys.

Dr. Lori is available to present, consult, and coach in several areas, such as:

- Project-Based Learning
- Technology Integration
- Instructional Coaching
- Critical Thinking
- Design Thinking/STEM/STEAM
- New-Teacher Induction
- Writer's Workshop
- Writing Across the Curriculum
- Comprehension
- Reading Across the Curriculum
- Independent Reading

Contact Dr. Lori for more information:

drlorielliott@gmail.com

https://drlorielliott.com

Twitter: @drlorielliott

Instagram: @drlorielliottedconsulting

Facebook: @drlorielliottedconsulting

MORE FROM DAVE BURGESS Consulting, Inc.

Since 2012, DBCI has been publishing books that inspire and equip educators to be their best. For more information on our titles or to purchase bulk orders for your school, district, or book study, visit DaveBurgessconsulting.com/DBCIbooks.

Like a PIRATE™ **Series**

More from the Like a PIRATETM Series
Teach Like a PIRATE by Dave Burgess
eXPlore Like a Pirate by Michael Matera
Learn Like a Pirate by Paul Solarz
Play Like a Pirate by Quinn Rollins
Run Like a Pirate by Adam Welcome
Tech Like a PIRATE by Matt Miller

Lead Like a PIRATE™

Lead Like a PIRATE by Shelley Burgess and Beth Houf
Balance Like a Pirate by Jessica Cabeen, Jessica Johnson, and Sarah Johnson
Lead beyond Your Title by Nili Bartley
Lead with Appreciation by Amber Teamann and Melinda Miller
Lead with Culture by Jay Billy
Lead with Instructional Rounds by Vicki Wilson
Lead with Literacy by Mandy Ellis

Leadership & School Culture

Culturize by Jimmy Casas
Escaping the School Leader's Dunk Tank by Rebecca Coda and Rick Jetter

Fight Song by Kim Bearden

From Teacher to Leader by Starr Sackstein

If the Dance Floor Is Empty, Change the Song by Joe Clark

The Innovator's Mindset by George Couros

It's OK to Say "They" by Christy Whittlesey

Kids Deserve It! by Todd Nesloney and Adam Welcome

Let Them Speak by Rebecca Coda and Rick Jetter

The Limitless School by Abe Hege and Adam Dovico

Live Your Excellence by Jimmy Casas

Next-Level Teaching by Jonathan Alsheimer

The Pepper Effect by Sean Gaillard

Principaled by Kate Barker, Kourtney Ferrua, and Rachael George

The Principled Principal by Jeffrey Zoul and Anthony McConnell

Relentless by Hamish Brewer

The Secret Solution by Todd Whitaker, Sam Miller, and Ryan Donlan

Start. Right. Now. by Todd Whitaker, Jeffrey Zoul, and Jimmy Casas

Stop. Right. Now. by Jimmy Casas and Jeffrey Zoul

Teachers Deserve It by Rae Hughart and Adam Welcome

Teach Your Class Off by CJ Reynolds

They Call Me "Mr. De" by Frank DeAngelis

Thrive through the Five by Jill M. Siler

Unmapped Potential by Julie Hasson and Missy Lennard

When Kids Lead by Todd Nesloney and Adam Dovico

Word Shift by Joy Kirr

Your School Rocks by Ryan McLane and Eric Lowe

Technology & Tools

50 Things You Can Do with Google Classroom by Alice Keeler and Libbi Miller

50 Things to Go Further with Google Classroom by Alice Keeler and Libbi Miller

140 Twitter Tips for Educators by Brad Currie, Billy Krakower, and Scott Rocco

Block Breaker by Brian Aspinall

Code Breaker by Brian Aspinall

The Complete EdTech Coach by Katherine Goyette and Adam Juarez

Control Alt Achieve by Eric Curts

The Esports Education Playbook, by Chris Aviles, Steve Isaacs, Christine Lion-Bailey, and Jesse Lubinsky

Google Apps for Littles by Christine Pinto and Alice Keeler

Master the Media by Julie Smith

Reality Bytes by Christine Lion-Bailey, Jesse Lubinsky, and Micah Shippee, PhD

Sail the 7 Cs with Microsoft Education by Becky Keene and Kathi Kersznowski

Shake Up Learning by Kasey Bell

Social LEADia by Jennifer Casa-Todd

Stepping up to Google Classroom by Alice Keeler and Kimberly Mattina

Teaching Math with Google Apps by Alice Keeler and Diana Herrington

Teachingland by Amanda Fox and Mary Ellen Weeks

Teaching Methods & Materials

All 4s and 5s by Andrew Sharos

Boredom Busters by Katie Powell

The Classroom Chef by John Stevens and Matt Vaudrey

The Collaborative Classroom by Trevor Muir

Copyrighteous by Diana Gill

CREATE by Bethany J. Petty

Ditch That Homework by Matt Miller and Alice Keeler

Ditch That Textbook by Matt Miller

Don't Ditch That Tech by Matt Miller, Nate Ridgway, and Angelia Ridgway

EDrenaline Rush by John Meehan

Educated by Design by Michael Cohen, The Tech Rabbi

The EduProtocol Field Guide by Marlena Hebern and Jon Corippo

The EduProtocol Field Guide: Book 2 by Marlena Hebern and
    Jon Corippo

Game On? Brain On! by Lindsay Portnoy, PhD

Innovating Play by Jessica LaBar-Twoemy and Christine Pinto

Instant Relevance by Denis Sheeran

LAUNCH by John Spencer and A.J. Juliani

Make Learning MAGICAL by Tisha Richmond

Pass the Baton by Kathryn Finch and Theresa Hoover

Pure Genius by Don Wettrick

The Revolution by Darren Ellwein and Derek McCoy

Shift This! by Joy Kirr

Skyrocket Your Teacher Coaching by Michael Cary Sonbert

Spark Learning by Ramsey Musallam

Sparks in the Dark by Travis Crowder and Todd Nesloney

Table Talk Math by John Stevens

Unpack Your Impact by Naomi O'Brien and LaNesha Tabb

The Wild Card by Hope and Wade King

The Writing on the Classroom Wall by Steve Wyborney

Inspiration, Professional Growth & Personal Development

Be REAL by Tara Martin

Be the One for Kids by Ryan Sheehy

The Coach ADVenture by Amy Illingworth

Creatively Productive by Lisa Johnson

Educational Eye Exam by Alicia Ray

The EduNinja Mindset by Jennifer Burdis

Empower Our Girls by Lynmara Colón and Adam Welcome

Finding Lifelines by Andrew Grieve and Andrew Sharos

The Four O'Clock Faculty by Rich Czyz

How Much Water Do We Have? by Pete and Kris Nunweiler

P Is for Pirate by Dave and Shelley Burgess

A Passion for Kindness by Tamara Letter

The Path to Serendipity by Allyson Apsey

Sanctuaries by Dan Tricarico

Saving Sycamore by Molly B. Hudgens

The SECRET SAUCE by Rich Czyz

Shattering the Perfect Teacher Myth by Aaron Hogan

Stories from Webb by Todd Nesloney

Talk to Me by Kim Bearden

Teach Better by Chad Ostrowski, Tiffany Ott, Rae Hughart, and Jeff Gargas

Teach Me, Teacher by Jacob Chastain

Teach, Play, Learn! by Adam Peterson

The Teachers of Oz by Herbie Raad and Nathan Lang-Raad

TeamMakers by Laura Robb and Evan Robb

Through the Lens of Serendipity by Allyson Apsey

The Zen Teacher by Dan Tricarico

Children's Books

Beyond Us by Aaron Polansky

Cannonball In by Tara Martin

Dolphins in Trees by Aaron Polansky

I Want to Be a Lot by Ashley Savage

The Princes of Serendip by Allyson Apsey

Ride with Emilio by Richard Nares

The Wild Card Kids by Hope and Wade King

Zom-Be a Design Thinker by Amanda Fox

Made in the USA
Las Vegas, NV
06 March 2021